I0091867

# Persuasive Attack

William L. Benoit, Kevin A. Stein, and
Matthew H. Barton

# Persuasive Attack

## Threatening Reputations in Public Discourse

PETER LANG

New York · Berlin · Bruxelles · Chennai · Lausanne · Oxford

Library of Congress Cataloging-in-Publication Data

Names: Benoit, William L., author. | Stein, Kevin A., author. |
Barton, Matthew H., author.
Title: Persuasive attack: threatening reputations in public discourse /
William L. Benoit, Kevin A. Stein, Matthew H. Barton.
Description: NewYork: Peter Lang, 2024. | Includes bibliographical
references.
Identifiers: LCCN 2024015316 | ISBN 9781636672144 (paperback) | ISBN
9783034350105 (hardback) | ISBN 9781636672120 (ebook) | ISBN
9781636672137 (epub)
Subjects: LCSH: Persuasion (Rhetoric) | Persuasion (Psychology) |
Reputation. | Social influence. | Attitude change.
Classification: LCC HM1196. B455 2024 | DDC 153.8/52—dc22
LC record available at https://lccn.loc.gov/2024015316
DOI 10.3726/b21906

Bibliographic information published by the Deutsche Nationalbibliothek.
The German National Library lists this publication in the German
National Bibliography; detailed bibliographic data is available
on the Internet at http://dnb.d-nb.de.

Cover design by William L. Benoit

ISBN 9781636672144 (paperback)
ISBN 9783034350105 (hardback)
ISBN 9781636672120 (ebook)
ISBN 9781636672137 (epub)
DOI 10.3726/b21906

© 2024 Peter Lang Group AG, Lausanne
Published by Peter Lang Publishing Inc., New York, USA
info@peterlang.com - www.peterlang.com

All rights reserved.
All parts of this publication are protected by copyright.
Any utilization outside the strict limits of the copyright law, without the permission of the
publisher, is forbidden and liable to prosecution.
This applies in particular to reproductions, translations, microfilming, and storage and
processing in electronic retrieval systems.

This publication has been peer reviewed.

## Dedication

This book is dedicated to the driving motivation in each of our lives. To Pam Benoit, Stacie Stein, and Carlynn Barton, thank you for encouraging us throughout this project. Bill would also like to thank Jennifer Benoit-Bryan for her support and for bringing United Breaks Guitars to his attention.

# ACKNOWLEDGMENTS

We would like to thank the editorial staff at Peter Lang Publishing for their help with the details of this project.

# CONTENTS

# Part I

## Introduction to Persuasive Attack

In our modern world, it is almost impossible to check a social media feed, a news outlet, or overhear a personal conversation without observing an attack on a person's character or behavior. However, not everyone's definition of persuasive attack is the same, nor is their understanding of the strategies and impacts of these attacks consistent. This book builds on the definition of persuasive attack as messages that criticize, denigrate, or vilify a target. Such attacks can be developed by people, groups, and/or organizations; in turn, these same entities can also be attacked. One missing voice in this conversation is the realization that there is an important interplay between attacks on behavior and attacks on character. Moreover, these distinctions have existed since the earliest chronicling of public discourse. This book offers a collection of diverse case studies to demonstrate that no examination of attack can be complete without adequately considering the relationship between attacks on behavior and attacks on character. The individual cases illustrate not only the strategies themselves but also the overall process for analyzing an attack, providing new insight for educators and students interested in this type of discourse.

In choosing appropriate cases to explore, we focused on medium (e.g., social media, television, cartoons, documentaries), history (from ancient to modern), type of public figure (e.g., politicians, athletes, actors, nation-states, institutions), and purpose behind attack (e.g., protect the innocent, protect our free time, advance social issues, hold public figures accountable). Although we considered several factors in the selection of cases, at the end of the day, we chose contexts that were interesting to us and that we believed would be interesting to those reading the book. The first chapter begins by explaining why persuasive attacks deserve scholarly attention. Next, it discusses where attack rhetoric fits in the broader landscape of persuasive communication and then reviews the literature in this area of research. This discussion is followed by an exploration of Attribution Theory and the Theory of Persuasive Attack. This introduction is followed by several case study chapters designed to help readers understand the nature of persuasive attacks in public discourse.

## The Importance of Persuasive Attack

The nature of persuasive attack is an important topic of investigation for several reasons. First, as Icks and Shiraev (2014) wrote about character assassination, "in every corner of history we find people of all ranks, occupations, and persuasions attempting to damage or destroy the reputation of their opponents in order to win political battles, discredit unwelcome news, or settle personal scores" (p. 3). Such attacks are inevitable in human society for four reasons. First, our world has limited resources. Only so much funding, material, space, or time is available. People can compete strenuously for these things, which means that the allocation of scarce resources can provoke the ire of those who desire a different distribution of resources. Second, factors that are beyond our control sometimes prevent people from meeting their obligations. Human behavior is frequently affected by circumstances, and the effects situations can have on our actions can provoke complaints from others. A third reason why attacks are so common is the fact that people are imperfect and at times commit wrongdoing, sometimes through honest mistakes, sometimes guided by their own self-interests. Fourth, people are individuals who embrace different priorities and competing goals. People may criticize those who impede our goals or those who do not help advance our goals. These four factors work together to ensure that actual or perceived wrongdoing is a common feature of human interaction. The vast pervasiveness of this phenomenon is a reminder that studying persuasive attacks in public discourse needs to be further explored.

Persuasive attacks can be false—that is, the attacker may know that the accusations in the attack are false—or true (of course, some statements are controversial and not easily classified as either true or false). Some attacks that are true can be beneficial to society, such as exposing the exploitation of child labor. False attacks are always reprehensible, but truthful criticisms can provide the audience with important information about the target. Also, people and society need to understand the nature of false attacks to prevent or reduce damage from such messages when they are inappropriate. Furthermore, a well-founded persuasive attack can help inform consumers or voters when they make choices; we need to know both the pros and cons of our choices before making decisions. Finally, a persuasive attack could make the attacker feel better, having vented their feelings. We never recommend that anyone make attacks that are false (that is, attacks that are believed to be false by the attacker) or even attacks that could be true but for which they have no support. We should not guess about wrongdoing or make up criticisms. Still, some attacks can actually be helpful.

## Attack as a Form of Persuasive Communication

Persuasive attack is best understood as a species of persuasive communication. Persuasion is a "process in which a source (the persuader) uses a message to achieve a goal by creating, changing, or reinforcing the attitudes of others (the audience)" (Benoit & Benoit, 2008, p.7). This assertion entails some important implications. A persuasive attack is intended to alter the audience's attitudes toward the target, creating new negative attitudes, diminishing positive attitudes, and/or changing existing attitudes from positive to negative. Fishbein and Ajzen (1975, 2010) developed the Theory of Reasoned Action, one of the key theories of attitude change or persuasion (see also Ajzen & Fishbein, 1980). An attitude is comprised of two elements: a belief and a value. Beliefs are observations about people, groups, places, things, ideas, or events. Beliefs are potentially verifiable (colloquially referred to as "facts"). A statement such as "Saturn has no solid core" is capable of verification, even if we cannot verify it at present. Values, in contrast to beliefs, are judgments of worth: good versus bad, beautiful versus ugly, pleasant versus unpleasant, desirable versus undesirable, nice versus nasty, and so forth. A statement such as "Saturn's rings are beautiful" is a judgment and not verifiable. Some values are accepted so completely by some people that they take these values as factual and true (e.g., "the Democratic Party is reprehensible" or "Republicans are abhorrent"), even though they are in fact controversial and not factual.

For a person to have an attitude, they must have both a belief and a value about the attitude object. For example, consider beliefs and values about candidates and political parties. If I have no preference (no value judgment) between the Democratic and Republican Parties, knowing (having a belief) that Candidate Thorne is a Republican or a Democrat cannot provide the basis for an attitude. Similarly, if I possess a value that favors one party over the other, but I do not know whether Candidate Thorne is a Republican or a Democrat, I cannot have an attitude toward this person based on their political party affiliation. Only if I have both a belief and a relevant value can I have an attitude toward Candidate Thorne.

Many attitudes are quite complex, encompassing several or many related belief + value pairs. These pairs can be all favorable, all unfavorable, or mixed. For example, I could have an attitude toward Frank comprised of these belief + value pairs:

1. Frank is helpful. It is important to be helpful to others.
2. Frank is honest. It is important to tell the truth.
3. Frank is friendly. I like friendly people.
4. Frank is educated. I like people who are well-educated.
5. Frank is funny. I like funny people.
6. Frank can be lazy at times. I do not like slothful people.

Most of these belief + value pairs are positive, inclining me to have a generally favorable attitude toward Frank. A persuasive attack could attempt to change my favorable attitude toward Frank in a variety of ways: Give me examples of times when Frank was not helpful (1. add belief); suggest that honesty must be tempered with compassion (2. diminish value); argue that a friendly appearance may not be sincere (3. create doubt about a belief); point out that Frank does not, in fact, have that much education (4. add belief); argue that being funny is not as important as other qualities (5. diminish value); and give more examples of Frank's laziness (6. add beliefs). As noted, some of these potential arguments concern beliefs, whereas others concern values. It would be easy to add more arguments where the persuader is trying to alter a belief or a value about Frank.

Furthermore, we could add new belief + value pairs that are unfavorable to Frank based on other elements of his character or actions. For example, you could tell me that Frank steals money from his family, an act you dislike. Of course, some of these approaches may not be persuasive, but they illustrate how understanding that an attitude is made up of belief + value pairs can help you develop ideas about how to persuade an audience and how to develop persuasive attacks.

Some attitudes are more polarized than others; such polarization can arise from several factors. Some beliefs are more important and, consequently, more firmly held than others. Naturally, attitudes based on more firmly held beliefs are likely more extreme than attitudes based on weaker ones. Furthermore, the more consistent the belief + value pairs (mostly or all positive—or mostly or all negative), the stronger and more polarized the attitude. This means a given attitude (such as a favorable attitude toward Sarah) can be easier to change in people who have a weaker attitude toward Sarah than in other people. It also underscores the idea that it is extremely important to understand a person's attitudes (beliefs and values) when trying to persuade that person.

Persuasive messages have limitations. A given message can be successful or unsuccessful. It is also likely that an attack will persuade some, but not all, of the audience (Benoit & Benoit, 2008). For example, a persuasive attack on a politician that would probably persuade many Republicans likely would not work with most Democrats, and vice versa. Persuasive attacks are not guaranteed to succeed, but surely we are better off when we understand how they work.

## Persuasive Attack Requires Division

A persuasive attack depends on division or fractures. One cannot plausibly criticize a person (or group or organization) if they are exactly the same as the potential attacker. Attacks on targets similar to the attacker would apply equally to the target and the attacker (this idea, however, does not stop all hypocritical criticisms). Divisions create opportunities for attacks. Our society has many fractures, such as differences in age, ethnicity, or gender. Today, a particularly prominent divide exists in political party affiliation. For example, in October 2020, President Trump's job approval was 95% among Republicans but only 3% for Democrats; Americans were very sharply divided (Gallup Poll, 2021a). Similarly, in October 2021, Joe Biden's approval rating was 4% in the GOP and 92% in the Democratic Party (Gallup Poll, 2021b). Not surprisingly, attacks by Republicans on Democrats and vice versa are a daily occurrence. This is particularly true during an election campaign, but partisan attacks occur at any time.

## Attacks on Policy and Character

A fundamental distinction in understanding persuasive attack is the difference between a person and his or her acts. Rountree (1995) notes the difference between actus (behavior, action, and policy) and status (nature, character, and personality) in political discourse. Of course, these two concepts are interrelated. People make inferences about a person's character from their actions (thinking that behavior reveals one's inner character). We also tend to assume that a person's basic personality influences their actions (believing character influences behavior). Still, these two concepts are conceptually distinct. In fact, content analysis of election messages has achieved high intercoder reliability for topics (policy versus character); this means that these concepts can be distinguished (see Benoit, 2007; 2014a, b). Thus, a persuasive attack can focus on the target's character, behavior, or both.

## Literature on Persuasive Attack

Persuasive attack has been a topic of research for at least 70 years. This review will examine rhetorical analyses of attacks, character assassination, narratives of blame, attacks in politics, reproaches in interpersonal communication, and the Theory of Persuasive Attack.

## Rhetorical Analyses of Persuasive Attack

Baskerville (1954) argued that Senator Joe McCarthy, who relentlessly attacked Communists, was a demagogue. He identified four methods employed by McCarthy to attack his targets: untruths and distortions, anti-intellectualism, oversimplification, and bogus documents. Baskerville also listed techniques used by past demagogues: sensationalism, exaggeration, oversimplification, or invective (note some overlap here). Again, this article is an interesting early investigation into persuasive attacks.

Scholars have investigated the nature of persuasive attacks in various ways. Bormann's (1972) Rhetorical Vision/Fantasy Theme Analysis was utilized to analyze political cartoons that attacked Bill Clinton (and others) in the Monica Lewinsky sex scandal (Benoit et al., 2001). Bostdorff (1987) employed ideas from Kenneth Burke to investigate political cartoons making fun of Secretary of the Interior James Watt: perspective by incongruity and the burlesque attitude. Benoit and Stein (2009) investigated recurrent themes in political cartoons about sexual abuse by Catholic priests.

King and Anderson (1971) (see also Raum & Measell, 1974) investigate the rhetoric of polarization as a genre (a collection of messages with similar features). Polarization is defined as a "process by which an extremely diversi-fied public is coalesced into two or more highly contrasting, mutually exclu-sive groups sharing a high degree of internal solidarity in those beliefs which the persuader considers salient" (p.244). In short, polarization seeks to divide the audience into (at least) two groups, usually "us" and "them." They found two basic strategies: affirmation (reinforcing the group that is "us") and sub-version (vilifying a common enemy, "them").

Ryan (1982) articulated the idea of *kategoria* and *apologia* as a "speech set" with a theoretical discussion and a case study. He proposed a typology of the possible components of persuasive attack (*kategoria*) based on Cicero's four stases. Stasis represents a point of disagreement between two parties; progress toward resolving a controversy is made until the people who are disagreeing reach a standstill, a place of disagreement. Cicero identified four points of stasis: fact (did something occur or does something exist?), definition (what is the meaning of that fact?), quality (what is the nature or severity of that fact?), and jurisdiction (what is the proper forum to discuss that fact?). Ryan also noted that attack and defense can occur on either character or policy (actions). He wrote a second case study (Ryan, 1984) and edited a collection of essays on *kategoria* and *apologia* (Ryan, 1988) to illustrate his ideas. Other approaches could provide the foundation for interesting analyses of persuasive attacks.

## Character Assassination

Davis (1950) developed an early approach to persuasive attack, calling it "character assassination." He investigated attacks on character in a variety of groups, including presidents, Jews, Negroes [sic], and labor union members. He also developed a list of forms of character assassination: name calling, guilt by association, transfer (from a person, group, or policy that is disliked to the target of attack), testimonials, fear appeals, double standard, stacking the deck (selecting the worst examples), bandwagon, hidden self-interest, and monopoly of media. One could quibble about individual strategies (e.g., whether guilt by association is different from transfer), but this was an important early treatment of persuasive attack.

More recent work has reinvigorated the study of character assassination. Icks and Shiraev (2014) edited a volume of essays on this topic. The chapters in this work were arranged chronologically; three chapters investigated character assassination in four eras: ancient Rome, the Middle Ages, early modern times, and contemporary times. Icks and Shiraev (2014) stipulate that for a message to be considered character assassination, it must be intentional and public. They also observed that an instance of character assassination can be "true or false, grossly exaggerated or mildly distorted" (p.6). They discussed several methods of attacking character: anonymous lies, misquoting, deleting information about the target, vandalism (e.g., defacing photographs or paintings), name-calling, and accusations of deviance. Samoilenko et al. (2020) edited a collection of theoretical essays and case studies of character assassination (see also Shiraev et al., 2022).

## Narratives of Blame

Seeger and Sellnow (2016) address what they label narratives of blame. They cite Kenneth Burke's (1984) three concepts of victimage, mortification, and transcendence. They discuss macro-level blame narratives, which transcend specific cases. They end by identifying two specific instances of blame narratives: Union Carbide's 1984 gas leak in Bhopal and
Conagra's salmonella contamination of chicken pot pies in 2007.

## Persuasive Attack in Political Communication

In the literature on political communication, Pfau and Kenski's *Attack Politics* (1990) offers "a theoretical and empirical examination of the role and impact of the attack message approach in modern political campaigns" (p.xv). Their analysis concerns three very general options: attacking first, counterattacking, and prevention (a refutation strategy). Jamieson's *Dirty Politics* (1992) discussed "Tactics of Attack." She identifies two major approaches: identification (association) and apposition (contrast): "to make their candidate's name a synonym for everything the electorate cherishes and to transform the opponent into an antonym of those treasured values" (p.47). She noted that each tactic can be further divided into verbal and visual aspects.

Benoit (2007, 2014a, b, & 2022a) and Benoit & Glantz (2020) articulated the Functional Theory of Political Campaign Discourse. This theory explains that political election messages enact three functions: acclaims (which are positive statements about the candidate; see Benoit, 1997), attacks (which are criticisms of opponents), and defenses (which are responses to, or refutations of, attacks). The concept of attack in Functional Theory is the same idea as persuasive attack. Benoit noted that attacks can occur on two topics: character (the personality and experience of the candidate) and policy (past and future proposals for governmental action and problems amenable to governmental action). Benoit and his colleagues have quantified the frequency of attack in a variety of candidate messages (e.g., candidate webpages, debates, TV ads, speeches, and candidates' social media, and direct mail advertising): messages in all three phases of an election campaign (primary, nominating convention, and general election), in campaigns for a variety of offices (e.g., president, chancellor, or prime minister; senator, member of the House of Representatives, governors, mayors), in the United States and abroad.

## Reproaches in Interpersonal Communication

Turning to the literature in relational communication, McLaughlin et al. (1983b) delineated four types of reproaches (statements that provoke accounts or apologies): (1) expressing surprise or disgust at the target; (2) suggesting that the target is inferior; (3) demanding an account; and (4) rebuking the target. Similarly, McLaughlin et al. (1983a) identified five strategies for eliciting accounts: projecting concession, excuse, justification, or refusal, and silence. Morris (1988) listed six ways to find fault with another person: "(1) formulating conduct as problematic; (2) accusing; (3) demanding explanations; (4) stopping present problematic conduct; (5) explaining stops; and (6) giving advisories" (p.9). Alberts (1988) conceptualized five categories of couples' complaints: "behavioral, performance, personal characteristic, personal appearance, and complaining" (p.187; see also Alberts, 1989). Vangelisti et al. (1991) articulated a group of strategies to induce feelings of guilt: "The most common verbal techniques for creating guilt in another were (a) stating relationship obligations, (b) enunciating sacrifice, (c) stating role obligations, (d) making comparisons, and (e) interrogating the other" (p.9). Sharkey (1992) listed six tactics used to provoke embarrassment (recognition, criticism or correction, tease, cause the target to appear unpoised, violation of privacy, and association; see also Cupach & Metts, 1990; Cupach et al., 1986; Metts & Cupach, 1989). These concepts help us understand the nature of persuasive attacks.

Garner (2009 & 2012) developed a list of ways to express dissent in organizations: ingratiation, direct factual appeals, exchange, circumvention, coalitions, pressure, inspiration, repetition, threatening resignation, solution presentation, venting, inspiration, and humor. These categories do not appear exhaustive (e.g., are indirect factual appeals possible?) or mutually exclusive (e.g., repetition appears to be a strategy that repeats one of the other strategies).

## Theory of Persuasive Attack

Benoit and Dorries (1996; see also Benoit, 2022b; Benoit & Harthcock, 1999; Castor, 2015, on accusatory discourse) developed a Theory of Persuasive Attack. Their theory was developed conceptually (rather than empirically identifying strategies observed in attacking messages), starting with an idea articulated by Pomerantz (1978). She explained that a complaint, which is another term for attack or criticism, consists of two key elements: identifying an act that appears offensive and placing blame or responsibility for that act. These two ideas (offensiveness and blame) clearly parallel Fishbein and Azjen's (2010) concepts of value and belief, respectively, discussed earlier. Benoit and Dorries described two groups of strategies for persuasive attack: attempts to increase the perceived responsibility of the target for an act and attempts to increase perceptions of the offensiveness of the act. As initially developed, this theory examined attacks (criticisms) of people, groups, and organizations based on behavior or actions (policy).

Legge et al. (2012) extended the Theory of Persuasive Attack, adding additional strategies (the victims were dignified, honorable, or noble; pejorative labeling; and identifying the target with an offensive value or ideology). They investigated attacks on talk radio host Rush Limbaugh after he demeaned Sandra Fluke, concluding that more of Limbaugh's criticism focused on the offensiveness of his statements than on his responsibility for these insults. DiSanza and Legge (2016) employed this typology to investigate Keith

Olbermann's attacks on the National Football League (NFL) and the Atlantic County district attorney (DA)'s office over the Ray Rice incident (a video tape showed Rice attacking his girlfriend, Janay Palmer). Stein et al. (2017) extended the work on persuasive attack to the realm of social media. In 2015, a member of the Communication Department at the University of Missouri, Melissa Click, became notorious when a video of her attempting to eject a student journalist covering a campus protest was made public. They report that these attacks focused on character rather than responsibility. Compton (2019) used the Theory of Persuasive Attack to analyze attacks on Stephen Colbert concerning his congressional testimony about farm labor issues. The theory of persuasive attack was extended in 2017 to include attacks on character or personality (Benoit, 2017, 2020; Benoit & Glantz, 2017).

Heider (1958) developed Attribution Theory, which investigates perceptions of the causes of human behavior. This theory advances a fundamental distinction between internal (personal) and external (situational) attribution. When we watch or are told about a person's behavior, do we infer that their actions stem from their basic nature (internal attribution) or from the situation in which they act (external attribution)? A persuasive attack must persuade the audience to believe that the target of the attack is responsible for the offensive act (internal attribution) and not, for example, situational factors (external attribution). Kelley (1967, 1971, 1972, and 1973) extended this work by explaining that internal (personal) attribution is more likely under three conditions:

1. High consistency: the target behaves the same way generally (so the behavior is likely a part of the person's personality).
2. High distinctiveness: The target's behavior differs in different situations (so the person is probably responsible for the actions).
3. Low consensus: the target's behavior is different from the actions of others (this behavior is not simply what everyone does; it occurs because of the target's nature).

Therefore, blame is more likely in these three circumstances. Jones and Davis (1965) developed attribution theory further by identifying other factors that influence attributions of responsibility for behavior. They identify five additional factors that guide the attribution of responsibility:

1. Intentions: If the target (apparently) intended to perform the behavior, the attribution should be internal; if the behavior seems accidental, the attribution should be external.
2. Choice: If the target chose to engage in the behavior, the attribution should be internal; if the target had no choice, the attribution should be external.
3. Social desirability: If the target engages in behavior that is considered undesirable by society, the attribution should be internal; behavior high in social desirability indicates external attribution (just following what others expect).
4. Hedonistic relevance: If the behavior benefits the target, the attribution should be internal; if the target does not benefit, external attribution is more likely.
5. Personalization: If the target's behavior seems to be aimed at us, internal attribution is more likely; if the behavior does not seem to be aimed at us, external attribution is more probable.

Furthermore, Attribution Theory concerns perceptions of human behavior, identifying factors that influence whether the audience (observers) infer that the target is responsible for offensive behavior (blame).

These ideas from Attribution Theory have clear implications for the Theory of Persuasive Attack (Coombs, 1995, 2012, and Stein & Ostrowsky, 2016, explain how attribution theory can inform image repair, which seeks to avoid internal attributions). Strategies for increasing blame include arguing that the accused performed the act before; this relates to both high consistency (the accused engaged in this behavior before) and high distinctiveness (the target of attack committed the act before across situations). Stressing that the accused planned the act is related to the Attribution Theory concept of intentional acts. Arguing that the accused knew the likely consequences of the act is similar to choice. The idea that the accused benefitted from the behavior is the same basic idea as hedonistic relevance. Consideration of Attribution Theory led to the addition of a new strategy for increasing blame: Others do not behave in this way (low consensus).

The Theory of Persuasive Attack declares that all criticisms of action have two elements in common: blame and offensiveness (see Pomerantz's [1978] analysis of complaints). Fishbein and Azjen's Theory of Reasoned Action (2010) provides a more general theoretical grounding: blame can usefully be considered to be a belief, and offensiveness can be seen as a value.

**Table 0.1.** Strategies of Persuasive Attack

| Strategies | Examples |
|---|---|
| **Intensifying Attacks on Actions** | |
| ***Increasing Perceived Responsibility*** | |
| Accused Committed the Act Before | "Accusations of an anti-Semitic rant are particularly damaging because the actor/director's [Mel Gibson], blockbuster 2004 film *The Passion of the Christ* was criticized by Jewish leaders as subtly placing blame on the Jews for the Crucifixion" (Stein, 2010). |
| Accused Planned the Act | "Brett and Mark came into the bedroom and locked the door behind them. There was music playing in the bedroom. It was turned up louder by either Brett or Mark once we were in the room" (Benoit & Stein, 2021). |
| Accused Knew the Likely Consequences of the Act | "They [tobacco industry] knew that the cigarette smoke was radioactive way back then and that it could potentially result in cancer, and they deliberately kept that information under wraps" (Jaslow, 2011). |
| Accused Benefitted from the Act | "*From Justin to Kelly* [film], a quickie attempt to wring a few more bucks from last year's American Idol finalists, is arguably the most insipid movie released so far this century" (Lumenick, 2003). |

*Continued*

*Table 0.1. Continued*

| Strategies | Examples |
|---|---|
| Others Do Not Act this Way | "A sign of an insecure human being is one who attacks others to make themselves feel better. I'm just sad that young kids have to see stupid Tweets like these and grow up thinking it's okay … Forget everything else Donald [Trump]. You're setting a bad example for kids. Our future" (Daniels, 2018). |
| Behavior Appears Aimed at Victim | "You coaches are crazy and you're screwing my kid …You don't know what you're doing. Adam James is the best player at the wide receiver position. If you've got the balls to call me back, and I don't think you do, call me back" (ESPN, 2010). |
| ***Increasing Offensiveness of Act*** | |
| Extent of the Damage | "I hate to use the word permanent, but we're [Exxon] here for a long time … The oil has now spread [after 9 days] over an area the size of Rhode Island, more than 1,000 square miles" (Peterson, 1989). |
| Persistence of Negative Effects | "She [Melissa Click] is why journalism is dying & racial tensions burgeoning" (Stein et al., 2017). |

Table 0.1. *Continued*

| Strategies | Examples |
|---|---|
| Effects on those the Audience Cares About | "It's not just a lack of preparedness [Bush administration response to Hurricane Katrina]. I think the easy answer is to say that there are poor people and black people and so government doesn't give a damn" (Purdum, 2005). |
| Inconsistency | "We don't begrudge a man for using Viagra any more than we resent women for using birth control. But fair is fair. If [Rush] Limbaugh is, in fact, using health insurance to purchase Viagra, he's a prostitute according to his own definition" (Legge et al., 2012). |
| Victims are Innocent/Helpless | "Feeding Our Future employees recruited individuals and entities to open Federal Child Nutrition Program sites throughout the state of Minnesota. These sites, created and operated by the defendants and others, fraudulently claimed to be serving meals to thousands of children a day within just days or weeks of being formed" (Rabinowitz & Jimenez, 2022). |

*Continued*

*Table 0.1. Continued*

| Strategies | Examples |
|---|---|
| Obligation to Protect Victims | "Really wish I hadn't seen that awful celebrity cover of Lennon's *Imagine*. The utter vacuity of extremely wealthy people thinking that will somehow bring hope versus pooling their wealth together to assist hard-hit fellow citizens or medical staff. Imagine doing that" (Saeed, 2020). |
| Victims are Dignified/Honorable/ Noble | "She [Sandra Fluke] was graceful, thoughtful, sincere, and brave. She is too kind, measured, and dignified to raise her voice in the blistering, full-throated rage that should come from the way she's been treated" (Legge et al., 2012). |
| Source (categories): Benoit & Dorries (1996) and Legge et al. (2012). | |
| **Intensifying Attacks on Character** | |
| ***Enhancing Perceptions that Accused Possesses Trait*** | |
| Accused has Performed Acts Consistent with Trait | "I always thought Kevin Spacey was a little too good at acting creepy. He wasn't acting all along" (Barton et al., 2020). |
| Accused has Made Statements Consistent with Trait | "Kanye west is a raging f***ing anti-Semite. His mental illness is not an excuse for his Neo-Nazi propaganda. I have friends who are bipolar. They don't suffer from vile bigotry and hate" (Thompson, 2022). |

*Table 0.1. Continued*

| Strategies | Examples |
|---|---|
| Accused Associates with People Who Share this Trait | "Liberal prof like Melissa Click are everywhere, imagine the things they tell students behind closed doors!" (Stein et al., 2017). |
| Accused is Contrasted with People Who Do Not Share this Trait | "Mr. Kavanaugh and Mr. Judge were extremely inebriated, they had clearly been drinking prior. And the other people at the party were not" (Benoit & Stein, 2021). |
| ***Enhancing Perceptions that Trait is Offensive*** | |
| Exemplify Trait with Offensive Example | "There is a type of film so bad that it is actually scary, like seeing those mawkish photographs of sweet little children in Victorian Britain dressed up as angels and realising after a few moments that they are corpses. Adam Sandler's new comedy *Jack and Jill* is such a film" (Bradshaw, 2012). |
| The Audience, or People They Care About, Can Be Hurt by this Trait | "[Odera] Odabi and his co-conspirators callously abused the trust of an elderly victim to line their pockets with millions in stolen cash. This office and our partners will work tirelessly to ensure that those who prey upon some of the most vulnerable members of our community are called to account for their crimes" (US Attorney's Office, Eastern District of NY, 2023). |
| Source (categories): Benoit (2020) and Benoit & Glantz (2017). | |

Paralleling the two main elements of a persuasive attack on behavior (blame and offensiveness), the two key elements of an attack on character are a belief that the target possesses a trait and a value that the trait is offensive (referring back to the belief/value pair). Both types of attacks have an offensive component. Table 0.1 lists the strategies for persuasive attack on actions (Benoit & Dorries, 1996; Legge et al., 2012), and identifies an additional category to this typology: victims are dignified, honorable, or noble. This table also includes strategies for persuasive attacks on character. Attacks on character argue that the target possesses an offensive trait or lacks an expected desirable trait. Illustrations of these categories in discourse can be found in Benoit and Dorries (1996), Benoit (2017, 2022b), or Benoit and Glantz (2017).

This book offers case studies across a variety of contexts to understand and illustrate the nature of persuasive attack. As observed earlier, attacks can be true or false (or controversial). The case studies in subsequent chapters are not meant to investigate whether the attacks identified are true or false, but rather the manner in which these strategies function in public discourse.

# References

Ajzen, I., & Fishbein, M. (1980). *Understanding attitudes and predicting social behavior.* Prentice-Hall.

Alberts, J. K. (1988). An analysis of couples' conversational complaints. *Communication Monographs, 55,* 184–197.

Alberts, J. K. (1989). A descriptive taxonomy of couples' complaint interactions. *Southern Speech Communication Journal, 54,* 125–143.

Barton, M. H., Stein, K. A., & Church, S. H. (2020). The disruptive power of memes: The carnivalesque and Kevin Spacey's place in the Weinstein moment. *Relevant Rhetoric, 2,* 1–21.

Baskerville, B. (1954). Joe McCarthy, brief - case demagogue. *Today's Speech, 2*(3), 8–15.

Benoit, W. L. (1995). *Accounts, excuses, apologies: A theory of image restoration strategies.* State University of New York Press.

Benoit, P. J. (1997). *Telling the success story: Acclaiming and disclaiming discourse.* State University of New York Press.

Benoit, W. L. (2007). *Communication in political campaigns.* Peter Lang.

Benoit, W. L. (2013). Mudslinging: The nature of attacks in political campaigns. In: C. Rountree (Ed.), *Venomous speech and other problems in American political discourse* (pp. 129–147). Praeger.

Benoit, W. L. (2014a). *Political election debates: Informing voters about policy and character.* Lexington Books.

Benoit, W. L. (2014b). *Seeing spots: A functional analysis of presidential television advertisements from 1952-2012* (2nd ed.). Lexington Books.

Benoit, W. L. (2015). *Accounts, excuses, apologies: A theory of image restoration strategies* (2nd ed.). State University of New York Press.

Benoit, W. L. (2017). Criticism of actions and character: Strategies for persuasive attack extended. *Relevant Rhetoric, 8,* 1–17.

Benoit, W. L. (2020). Character assassination and persuasive attack on CBS's Face the Nation. In S. A. Samoilenko, M. Icks, J. Keohane, & E. Shiraev, E. (Eds.), *Routledge handbook of character assassination and reputation management* (pp. 295–306). Routledge.

Benoit, W. L. (2021). Image Repair Theory. In W. Johansen & F. Frandsen (Eds.), *Handbook of crisis communication* (pp. 105–119). Mouton de Gruyter.

Benoit, W. L. (2022a). *Communication in political campaigns: A functional analysis of election messages* (2nd ed.). Peter Lang.

Benoit, W. L. (2022b). Persuasive attack on President Donald Trump and President Vladimir Putin. *Discourse & Communication, 16,* 621–631.

Benoit, W. L., & Benoit, P. J. (2008). *Persuasive messages: Balancing influence in communication.* Blackwell.

Benoit, W. L., & Dorries, B. (1996). Dateline NBC's persuasive attack on Wal-Mart. *Communication Quarterly, 44,* 464–477.

Benoit, W. L., & Glantz, M. (2017). *Persuasive attack on Donald Trump in the 2016 Republican primaries.* Lexington Books.

Benoit, W. L., & Glantz, M. (2020). *Presidential campaigns in the age of social media: Clinton and Trump.* Peter Lang.

Benoit, W. L., & Harthcock, A. (1999). Attacking the tobacco industry: A rhetorical analysis of advertisements by The Campaign for Tobacco-Free Kids. *Southern Communication Journal, 65,* 66–81.

Benoit, W. L, Klyukovski, A. A., McHale, J. P., & Airne, D. (2001). A fantasy theme analysis of political cartoons on the Clinton-Lewinsky-Starr affair. *Critical Studies in Mass Communication, 18*(4), 377-394.

Benoit, W. L., & Stein, K. A. (2009). The pope looks forward as he looks back: An analysis of political cartoons during the Catholic sexual abuse scandal. In J. R. Blaney & J. P. Zompetti (Eds). *The Rhetoric of John Paul.* Rowman and Littlefield.

Benoit, W. L., & Stein, K. A. (2021). Character assassination on Judge Brett Kavanaugh in his 2018 Supreme Court confirmation hearing. *Journal of Applied Social Theory, 1,* 7–30.

Boklan, S., Griffin, D. J., & Goodboy, A. K. (2014). Communicating consumer complaints: Message content and its perceived effectiveness. *Communication Quarterly, 62,* 357–380.

Bormann, E.G. (1972). Fantasy and rhetorical vision: The rhetorical criticism of social reality. *Quarterly Journal of Speech 58,* 396-407.

Bradshaw, P. (2012, June 18). Review - Transformers: Revenge of the Fallen. *The Guardian.* https://www.theguardian.com/film/2009/jun/19/transformers-revenge-of-the-fallen-megan-fox-michael-bay

Burke, K. (1984). *Attitudes toward history.* University of California Press.

Castor, T. (2015). Accusatory discourse. In K. Tracy (Ed.), *The international encyclopedia of language and social interaction* (pp. 1–5). John Wiley & Sons.

Compton, J. (2019). Late night television comedy, mid-afternoon congressional testimony: Attacks on Stephen Colbert's House Judiciary Committee appearance. *Comedy Studies, 10*, 145–153.

Coombs, W. T. (1995). Choosing the right words: The development of guidelines for the selection of "appropriate" crisis-response strategies. *Management Communication Quarterly, 8*, 447–476.

Coombs, W. T. (1998). An analytic framework for crisis situations: Better responses from a better understanding of the situation. *Journal of Public Relations Research, 10*, 177–191.

Coombs, W. T. (2012). *Ongoing crisis communication: Planning, managing, and responding* (3rd ed.). Sage.

Cupach, W. R., & Metts, S. (1990). Remedial processes in embarrassing predicaments. In J. A. Anderson (Ed.), *Communication Yearbook* (Vol. 12, pp. 323–352). Sage.

Cupach, W. R., Metts, S., & Hazelton, V. (1986). Coping with embarrassing predicaments: Remedial strategies and their perceived utility. *Journal of Language and Social Psychology, 5*, 181–200.

Daniels, T. (2018, August 4). Sports world reacts to Donald Trump ripping LeBron James' intelligence. *Bleacher Report.* bleacherreport.com/articles/2789464-sports-world-reacts-to-donald-trump-ripping-lebron-james-intelligence

Davis, J. (1950). *Character Assassination.* Philosophical Library.

DiSanza, J. R., & Legge, N. J. (2016). The rhetoric of persuasive attack: Continuing the development of a taxonomy of attack strategies and tactics. *Relevant Rhetoric, 7*, 1–16.

ESPN (2010, January 15). Suit alleges phone calls by James' father. https://www.espn.com/college-football/news/story?id=4828405

Fishbein, M., & Ajzen, I. (1975). *Belief, attitude, intention, and behavior.* Addison-Wesley.

Fishbein, M., & Ajzen, I. (2010). *Predicting and changing behavior: The reasoned action approach.* Psychology Press.

Gallup Poll. (2021a). Donald Trump's job approval by party identification. https://news.gallup.com/poll/203198/presidential-approval-ratings-donald-trump.aspx

Gallup Poll. (2021b). Joe Biden's job approval by party identification. https://news.gallup.com/poll/329384/presidential-approval-ratings-joe-biden.aspx

Garner, J. T. (2009). When things go wrong at work: An exploration of organizational dissent messages. *Communication Studies, 60*, 197–218.

Garner, J. T. (2012). Making waves at work: Perceived effectiveness and appropriateness of organizational dissent messages. *Management Communication Quarterly, 26*, 224–240.

Heider. F (1958). *The psychology of interpersonal relations.* Wiley.

Icks, M., and Shiraev, E. (2014). Introduction. In M. Ickes & E. Shiraev (Eds.), *Character assassination throughout the ages* (pp. 1–13). Palgrave.

Jamieson, K. H. (1992). *Dirty politics: Deception, distraction, and democracy.* Oxford University Press.

Jaslow, R. (2011, September 30). Big tobacco kept cancer risk in cigarettes secret: Study. *CBS News.* https://www.cbsnews.com/news/big-tobacco-kept-cancer-risk-in-cigarettes-secret-study/

Jones, E. E., & Davis, K. E. (1965) From acts to dispositions: The attribution process in social psychology. In L. Berkowitz (Ed.), *Advances in experimental social psychology* (Vol. 2, pp. 219–266), Academic Press.

Kelley, H. H. (1967). Attribution theory in social psychology. *Nebraska Symposium on Motivation, 15*, 192–238.

Kelley, H. H. (1971). *Attribution and the attribution process*. General Learning Press.

Kelley, H. H. (1972). *Causal schemata and the attribution process*. General Learning Press.

Kelley, H. H. (1973). The processes of causal attribution. *American Psychologist, 28*, 107–128.

King, A. A., & Anderson, F. D. (1971). Nixon, Agnew, and the "Silent Majority": A case study in the rhetoric of polarization. *Western Speech, 35*, 243–255.

Legge, N. J., DiSanza, J. R., Gribas, J., & Shiffler, A. (2012). "He sounded like a vile, disgusting pervert…" An analysis of persuasive attacks on Rush Limbaugh during the Sandra Fluke controversy. *Journal of Radio & Audio Media, 19*, 173–205.

Lumenick, L. (2003, June 21). American idull. *New York Post*. https://nypost.com/2003/06/21/american-idull/

McLaughlin, M. L., Cody, M. J., & O'Hair, H. D. (1983a). The management of failure events: Some contextual determinants of accounting behavior. *Human Communication Research, 9*, 208–224.

McLaughlin, M. L., Cody, M. J., & Rosenstein, N. E. (1983b). Account sequences in conversations between strangers. *Communication Monographs, 50*, 102–125.

Metts, S., & Cupach, W. R. (1989). Situational influence on the use of remedial strategies in embarrassing predicaments. *Communication Monographs, 56*, 151–162.

Morris, G. H. (1988). Finding fault. *Journal of Language and Social Psychology, 7*, 1–25.

Peterson, C. (1989, April 3). Coast Guard faults plans to contain spill. *Washington Post*, p. A17.

Pfau, M., & Kenski, H. C. (1990). *Attack politics: Strategy and defense*. Praeger.

Pomerantz, A. (1978). Attributions of responsibility: Blamings. *Sociology, 12*, 115–121.

Purdum, T. S. (2005, September 3). Across U.S., outrage at response. *The New York Times*, p. 1.

Rabbinowitz, H., & Jimenez, O. (2022, September 20). Feeding our future fraud: $250M stolen from program providing meals to low-income kids, 47 charged. *ABC 7 Eyewitness News*. https://abc7chicago.com/feeding-our-future-fraud-mn-aimee-bock-minnesota-covid-19-pandemic/12243777/

Raum, R. D., & Measell, J. S. (1974). Wallace and his ways: A study of the rhetorical genre of polarization. *Central States Speech Journal, 25*, 28–35.

Rokeach, M. (1968). *Beliefs, attitudes, and values: A theory of organization and change*. Jossey-Bass.

Rokeach, M. (1973). *The nature of human values*. Free Press.

Rountree, J. C. (1995). The president as God, The recession as evil: Actus, status, and the president's rhetorical bind in the 1992 election. *Quarterly Journal of Speech, 81*, 325–352.

Ryan, H. R. (1982). Kategoria and apologia: On their rhetorical criticism as a speech set. *Quarterly Journal of Speech, 68*, 256–261.

Ryan, H. R. (1984). Baldwin vs. Edward VIII: A case study in *kategoria* and *apologia*. *Southern Speech Communication Journal, 49*, 125–134.

Ryan, H. R. (1988). *Oratorical encounters: Selected studies and sources of twentieth-century political accusations and apologies*. Greenwood Press.

Saeed, S. (2020, March 19). *Twitter*. https://twitter.com/SanaSaeed/status/124071101301 3557250

Samoilenko, S. A., Icks, M., Keohane, J., & Shiraev, E. (Eds.). (2020). *Routledge handbook of character assassination and reputation management*. Routledge.

Seeger, M. W., & Sellnow, T. L. (2016). *Narratives of crisis: Telling stories of ruin and renewal*. Stanford Business Press.

Sharkey, W. F. (1992). Use and responses to intentional embarrassment. *Communication Studies, 43*, 257–275.

Shiraev, E. B., Keohane, J., Icks, M., & Samoilenko, S. A. (2022). *Character assassination and reputation management: Theory and applications*. Routledge.

Stein, K. A. (2010). Jewish *antapologia* in response to Mel Gibson's multiple attempts at absolution. *Relevant Rhetoric, 1*, 1–14.

Stein, K. A., Barton, M. H., & Paul, W. B. (2017). 140 characters to say "I hate you": Melissa Click, racism, and the media circus at Mizzou. *Relevant Rhetoric, 8*, 1–15.

Stein, K. A., Barton, M. H., & Turman, P. D. (2013). In the dark at Texas Tech: News coverage involving the image repair discourse of Mike Leach and Adam James. In J. R. Blaney, L. R. Lippert, & J. S. Smith (Eds.) Repairing the athlete's image (pp. 203-222): Lanham, MD: Lexington Books (Rowman & Littlefield).

Stein, K. A., & Ostrowsky, M. K. (2016). "Taco the puppy is super sick": Student excuses as a unique form of apologia rhetoric. *Relevant Rhetoric, 7*, 1-19.

Thompson, E. (2022, December 11). Reese Witherspoon, Florence Pugh and more stand against anti-Semitism after Kanye West controversy. *US Weekly*. https://www.usmagazine.com/ celebrity-news/pictures/celebs-speak-out-against-anti-semitism-amid-kanye-controversy/

US Attorney's Office, Eastern District of New York (2023, April 25). Georgia man indicted for scheme to defraud elderly Suffolk County victim of more than $5 million. *Justice.gov*. https://www.justice.gov/usao-edny/pr/georgia-man-indicted-scheme-defraud-elderly-suff olk-county-victim-more-5-million

Vangelisti, A. L., Daly, J. A., & Rudnick, J. R. (1991). Making people feel guilty in conversations: Techniques and correlates. *Human Communication Research, 18*, 3–39.

# Part II
## POP CULTURE

# PERSUASIVE ATTACK IN MEMES ON MELANIA TRUMP AND TOM BRADY

Memes have emerged as an important vehicle for creating shared culture in contemporary society (Shifman, 2014). A meme has been defined as "an idea, behavior, style, or usage that spreads from person to person within a culture" ("Munson," 2022, para. 4). Dawkins (1976) originally coined the term "meme" by drawing a comparison between a biological "gene" and a sociological "meme," wherein a meme "functions in a mind the same way a gene or virus functions in the body" (p.249). More recently, Milner (2016) argued:

> Internet memes take the form of pictures captioned on Reddit, puns hashtagged on Twitter, and videos mashed up on YouTube. They can be widely shared catchphrases, Auto-Tuned songs, manipulated stock photos, or recordings of physical performances. They are used to make jokes, argue points, and connect friends. (p.1)

Memes can be disseminated through any medium, including graffiti spray-painted on walls, but the Internet and social media make it extremely easy for memes to move quickly through the population. Ideas swim around in the meme pool of human society, "infecting" people, replicating, and mutating as they travel.

To illustrate the idea of memes, in February 2021, as the state of Texas suffered from power outages in the midst of freezing temperatures, Senator Ted

Cruz (R, TX) took his family to a resort in Cancun (see, e.g., Goldmacher & Fandos, 2021). One manifestation of the outpouring of outrage at his actions was a series of memes. Many were based on a photograph of Senator Cruz with a small suitcase at the airport during his trip. One meme showed Cruz with his suitcase on a beach with Chris Christie and his wife, Mary Pat Christie. Another version of this meme featured the Christies, Cruz, and bundled-up Bernie Sanders (sitting at Biden's Inauguration) together at the beach. Other memes depicted Cruz and his suitcase in front of a section of the border wall, on Mars, at the Battle of the Alamo, in the midst of the Normandy landing in WWI, at Pearl Harbor in WWII, behind Baby Yoda, at ground zero on 9/11, at the January 6, 2021, insurrection with the man wearing a coonskin cap and antlers, and in the background at Mount Sinai when the 10 tablets were revealed to Moses (see "20 photos [hops] from Ted Cruz," 2021). Memes repeatedly slammed Cruz over his Cancun vacation.

Meme 1: Ted Cruz, Bernie Sanders, Chris and Mary Pat Christie at the beach
Source: https://www.dailymail.co.uk/news/article-9275289/Twitter-goes-frenzy-Ted-Cruz-Cancun-trip-memes.html

These examples illustrate how memes mutate, as Cruz was depicted in a series of silly situations, implying that Cruz running away to Cancun during this crisis was as ridiculous as if he had traveled to other absurd destinations. This meme could (and may have) mutated in a different direction, showing other people with similar suitcases, suggesting they were, like Cruz, running away from their responsibilities. The example above shows how different memes can intersect, with the Christies, Sanders, and Cruz "gathering" together at the beach.

Some memes are innocuous, nothing more than simple fun. For example, a commercial for Dos Equis beer features a distinguished-looking man labeled "The most interesting man in the world" ("Know your meme," 2021). He observed that he does not always drink beer, but when he does, he chooses Dos Equis. This idea has spawned a multitude of memes, many based on a picture of the actor in this commercial: "I don't always use Internet Explorer … but when I do, it's to download a different browser." This meme clearly attacks Microsoft's web browser, Internet Explorer. Another meme reports that "I don't always go to McDonalds … But when I do, I'm loving it," echoes a marketing slogan from a McDonald's commercial. A person admits that "I don't always have a valid argument … But when I do, it's later that day, in the shower." Each iteration demonstrates how the original meme mutates as it propagates. One meme includes a picture of Melania Trump with the caption, "I don't always say nice things about my husband … But when I do, I like to pretend my husband is Barack Obama." Given the fact that Donald Trump is not known for his admiration of Barack Obama, this is a sharp slam. The Internet also has a variety of memes about such topics as cats, puppies, and Baby Yoda.

Other memes, however, are intended to criticize and attack a target (we do not claim that memes can serve only two purposes; clearly, they can inform viewers about cultural events). When a persuasive attack embodied in a meme mutates and spreads across the Internet, this symbolic movement increases the potential influence of that attack. Attacks in memes often feature an image and text, which renders them similar to political cartoons (see Benoit & Glantz, 2017). Barton et al. (2020) liken the idea of memes to "parody, because of their silliness, snark, and overall comic tone, memes are a modern version of the *carnivalesque*" (p.6). Just as political cartoons make use of commonplaces and current topics, memes work because they consist of "families, stock characters, and templates duplicated many times by many different people, united by similar content and characteristics" (Barton et al., 2020, p.5). They explain that we would do well to investigate memes "because they are the language of the contemporary online world" (p.4). Some memes wither and die on the Internet; others become viral.

This chapter investigates memes as vehicles for persuasive attacks. It examines memes in two contexts: Melania Trump's plagiarism of a speech by

Michelle Obama and the football "Deflategate" scandal of Tom Brady and the New England Patriots. The idea here is not to provide an exhaustive examination of these topics but rather to illustrate the idea that some memes can be usefully understood as instances of persuasive attack.

## Memes about Melania Trump's Plagiarism of Michelle Obama

On July 18, 2016, Melania Trump delivered a speech at the Republican National Convention, where her husband, Donald Trump, would soon be nominated as the Grand Old Party (GOP) presidential candidate. Questions arose about whether part of Melania Trump's speech had been copied (plagiarized) from a speech given by Michelle Obama in 2008 before her husband received the Democratic presidential nomination. Several reports displayed similar passages from these two speeches (e.g., BBC, 2016). Not surprisingly, in contemporary culture, memes erupted on the Internet about this accusation. This chapter does not attempt to assess the importance or appropriateness of this criticism (ironically, during the 1988 Democratic primary campaign, Joe Biden was accused of several instances of plagiarism; see, e.g., Satija, 2019). These memes were creative (see, e.g., Kurtzman, 2020); they were likely considered funny by many, but not all, of the audience.

One meme showed a photograph of Melania Trump at a microphone. The top line called her Melania Vanilli Trump (alluding to pop duo Milli Vanilli, who endured a scandal for appropriating the music of others; see Bailey, 2019). The bottom of this meme included a mashup of well-known sayings allegedly spoken by Melania Trump: "Ask not what our country can do for you but I have a dream from four score and seven years ago that blessed are the poor in spirit […]." One meme also "credits" Melania Trump with several other notable sayings: "There is nothing to fear but fear itself" (FDR), "Winter is coming" (*Game of Thrones*), "That's one small step for man, one giant leap for mankind" (Neil Armstrong), and "I do not like green eggs and ham. I do not like them, Sam-I-Am" (Dr. Seuss). Notice how this meme runs the gamut of contexts: politics, television, space, and children's literature. The idea of Trump allegedly appropriating other absurd statements appears in other memes: "Luke: I am your father" (*Star Wars*), "I am so proud of my amazing black daughters, Sasha and Malia" (Michelle Obama's daughters), and "I have a dream" (Martin Luther King Jr.). Again, these statements obviously did not originate from Melania Trump (to make it perfectly clear, Melania Trump did not say these, but she was ridiculed by jokingly attributing these preposterous statements to her). One meme clearly used Photoshop to insert Melania Trump's face onto Michelle Obama's body in an Obama family photo with Sasha, Barack, and Malia. Another meme has a photo of Milli Vanilli with the legend "Melania's Speech Writers," showing that memes can jab a target from opposite directions.

Another variation referred to cutting (Ctrl-C) and pasting (Ctrl-V) with a computer. One meme depicted Melania behind a microphone saying, "I want to thank my trusted speech writers: Ctrl-C and Ctrl-V." Another one showed what was purported to be Melania Trump's keyboard, which only had three keys (Ctrl, C, and V).

The keyboard used to write her speech
#FamousMelaniaTrumpQuotes 😂😂

Meme 2: Melania Trump's Keyboard
Source: https://www.liveabout.com/funniest-melania-trump-memes-4064562

This meme takes advantage o our familiarity with both a computer keyboard and the commands Ctrl-C and Ctrl-V.

Some memes managed to attack both Melania Trump and Donald Trump. A meme had a picture of Donald Trump with the caption, "Slovenia doesn't send their best. They send liars, plagiarists, and thieves. And some, I assume, are beautiful women" (Melania Trump was born in Slovenia).

"Slovenia doesn't send their best.
They send liars, plagiarists, and thieves.
And some, I assume, are beautiful women."

Meme 3: Slovenia sends liars, plagiarists, and thieves
Source: https://www.liveabout.com/funniest-melania-trump-memes-4064562

Clearly, using the word "plagiarists" activates the accusation of Melania Trump's plagiarism. This declaration echoes a statement by Donald Trump that some considered racist: Trump's campaign speech declared that Mexico is "sending people that have a lot of problems, and they're bringing those problems with them. They're bringing drugs. They're bringing crime. They're rapists. And some, I assume, are good people." Another meme shows photos of Melania and Donald Trump, reporting that her "Speech Writing Degree" was from "Trump University." This message alludes to both Melania Trump's plagiarism and Donald Trump's failed university (Donald Trump settled lawsuits from students of Trump University for US$25 million; Hafner, 2018). These memes demonstrate the creativity of using memes to attack a target.

## Memes about the New England Patriots "Deflategate" Scandal

After the 2014 AFC (American Football Conference), in which the New England Patriots defeated the Indianapolis Colts, 45-7, allegations arose about cheating in the game. Patriots quarterback Tom Brady was accused of having "ordered the deliberate deflation of footballs used in the Patriots' victory" ("Deflategate," 2021). NFL rules stipulate that all footballs must be inflated to a pressure between 12.5 and 13.5 psi (pounds per square inch). The amount of pressure in a football matters because "removing air from a football makes it easier to grip, throw, and catch" ("Deflategate," 2021). Each team supplied footballs for use in this game. At halftime, game officials checked the air pressure in these footballs: "Five of eleven [Patriot] footballs were measured below 11.0 pounds, this being less than 90% of the officially mandated minimum pressure" ("Deflategate," 2021). These balls were re-inflated to the proper pressure before the second half. New England won this football game. It seems clear that this is an instance of cheating; whether the underinflated balls made a difference in this game is not as clear (in the first half, the Patriots led 17-7 in the second half; with balls properly inflated, the Patriots outscored the Colts 28-0 in the second half; "Deflategate," 2021). The NFL imposed penalties for this scandal, fining New England US$1 million, removing two future draft picks, and suspending Brady for four games. Appeals over these penalties ultimately failed ("Deflategate," 2021). Not surprisingly, some football fans delighted in ridiculing the Patriots and Brady over these accusations ("Best New England Patriots," 2021).

One meme depicted a Wheaties cereal box, which famously puts exceptional athletes on its cover and declares itself the "Breakfast of Champions," with both Brady and Belichick featured as "Cheaties" and promoting the cereal as the "Breakfast of Chumps."

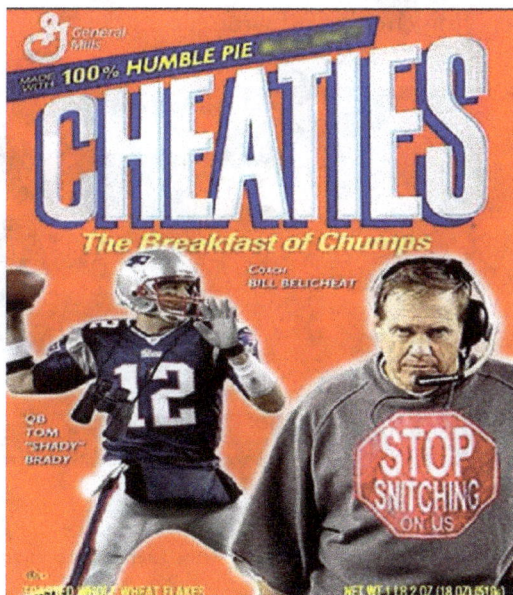

Meme 4: Cheaties
Source: https://www.liveabout.com/new-england-patriots-deflategate-memes-1923793

The idea that the Patriots were cheaters appeared in a meme about Coach Belichick: "Deflaters gonna deflate," alluding to the saying that "Cheaters gonna cheat." This went beyond saying the Patriots cheated in this game, indicating that by nature (character) they were cheaters. One meme suggested that Belichick looking out in a hoodie was Emperor Palpatine from Star Wars: "Let the hate flow through you." This was not a favorable characterization of the New England head coach. Another meme showed quarterback Tom Brady hugging a football. The caption explained that "I love football so much, I just must've hugged the psi right out of it." Obviously, this is not why these footballs were underinflated. Several memes took the opportunity to make puns on the word "balls." Brady was shown declaring, "When I felt the balls, they were perfect." This idea was echoed in another meme, mimicking Brady on a tabloid cover: "My balls are perfect." Another meme depicted Patriot's head coach Bill Belichick taunting critics: "Go ahead. Weigh my balls." Brady was shown whispering to Belichick. "Do you know what I like, coach? Soft balls." These memes all clearly attacked Brady, Belichick, and the New England Patriots.

Another image depicted Pinocchio with a long wooden nose, indicating that Brady was lying (he denied wrongdoing).

Meme 5: Pinocchio
Source: https://www.liveabout.com/new-england-patriots-deflategate-memes-1923793

One meme purported to show the 12th football player speaking at a press conference: "I am the 12$^{th}$ ball, and I'm here to clear my name. I had no idea what the other 11 balls were doing … Please respect my family's privacy." The request to "respect my family's privacy" adds a bit of silliness to the attack. Two memes used images of deflated footballs to criticize this football team. One showed a partially deflated football on the Vince Lombardi trophy (awarded to the Super Bowl winner).

Meme 6: Lombardi trophy
Source: https://www.liveabout.com/new-england-patriots-deflategate-memes-1923793

This meme reinforced the attack on the Patriots, altering the football on the Lombardi Trophy to appear deflated. Another meme altered a famous painting by Salvador Dali, "The Persistence of Memory." Melted clocks were replaced by melted (deflated) footballs. This "painting" was signed by Belichick rather than Dali.

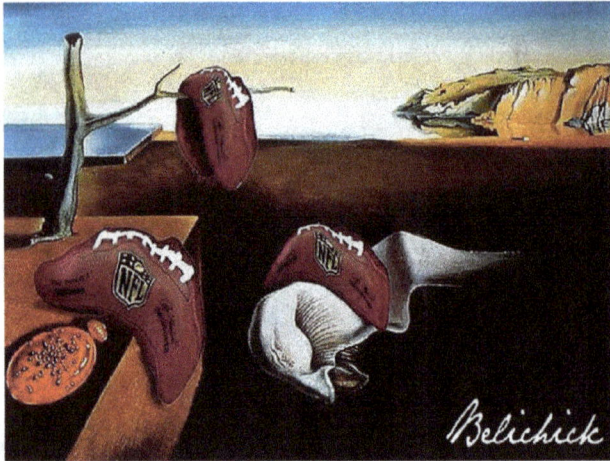

Meme 7: Salvadore Dali melting footballs
Source: https://www.liveabout.com/new-england-patriots-deflategate-memes-1923793

These memes also employed popular culture to criticize the New England Patriots.

An unusual meme on Deflategate defended the Patriots. It depicted Tom Brady recounting, "We scored 14 points with deflated footballs and 28 points with inflated footballs. I'm just so glad someone found the problem." The implication here is that New England would have done even better if the footballs had been properly inflated for both the first and second halves.

## Observations and Conclusions

This analysis illustrates that there are a variety of channels through which attacks can be disseminated. Although memes are often viewed as superficial forms of entertainment, previous studies have established that memes are much more than humorous diversions (Barton et al., 2020; Taylor et al., 2023). In fact, memes provide biting social commentary on individual character as well as behavior and allow attacks to remain present in the public consciousness for longer periods of time. Because memes are simple to create, share, and digest, they can become a social tinderbox that is easy to ignite and incredibly difficult to extinguish. They frequently make use of cultural knowledge (e.g., Ctrl-C and Ctrl-V, of Pinocchio, of Salvador Dali, of Wheaties) to make attacks. This shared knowledge is important to creating meaning in these short messages; e.g., a meme does not have to say "Tom Brady is a liar" when it depicts him as Pinocchio. Many memes can be considered visual metaphors, relying on a metaphor to create meaning. However, because memes rely mostly on imagery and very few words, the attack strategies are more difficult to articulate by the attacker and interpret by the audience. That being said, an examination of these types of attacks demonstrates how these various strategies can be used not only within this particular medium but also within the larger scope of persuasive attack in public.

Not surprisingly, in this case, we did not see instances of strategies for enhancing blame or offensiveness. The memes with repeated instances of (fake) plagiarism attributed to Melania Trump are not the same thing as arguing that the target repeated the offense. In other words, the memes examined here did not claim that *she* plagiarized repeatedly. Had that been the case, the attack would have been stronger because generally, people who make the same mistakes over and over have a more flawed character than a person with a singular lapse in judgment. For example, consider the use of the extent of damage as a way to increase offensiveness against both of these people. In these memes, the Trumps are attacked using this strategy to transform plagiarism from a minimal offense to an outright deception. Similarly, Tom Brady was discursively demoted from a future Hall of Fame athlete to a cheating chump. By extension, this entire line of attack is meant to completely destroy credibility.

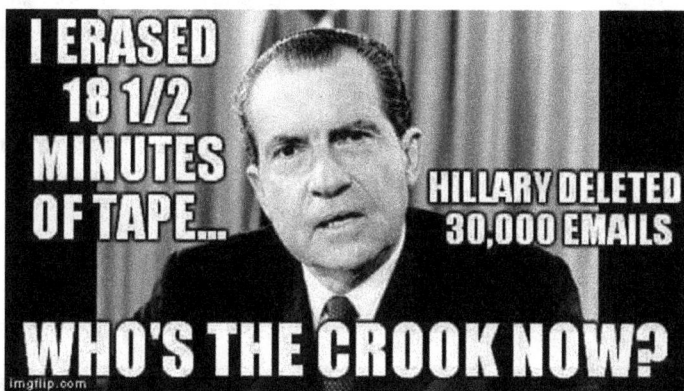

Meme 8: Hillary Clinton: Who is the crook?
Source: https://imgur.com/gallery/ladies-gentlemen-i-present-to-you-richard-tricky-nixon-presented-to-you-by-great-taste-of-charleston-chew-MEUxT

Meme 9: Trump and Coronavirus
Source: https://x.com/oldschoolprogr1/status/1767558226474570078

Memes can and do employ strategies for enhancing persuasive attack, and this analysis shows that our contribution to current theory enhances knowledge in areas of new communication platforms. However, messages that are intentionally brief, such as most memes, offer less opportunity for their authors to make deep and enduring arguments that are capable of sustained damage (e.g., from simple credibility loss to destruction of livelihood to criminal charges), whether that is a Super Bowl-winning quarterback or the nation's first lady. In sum, memes are becoming an important contemporary means of persuasive attack.

# References

Bailey, J. (2019, September 4). Retrospective: 30 years since Milli Vanilli. *Plagiarism Today*. https://www.plagiarismtoday.com/2019/09/04/retrospective-30-years-since-milli-vanilli/

Barton, M. H., Stein, K. A., & Church, S. H. (2020). The disruptive power of memes: The carnivalesque and Kevin Spacey's place in the Weinstein moment. *Relevant Rhetoric*, *11*, 1–21.

BBC. (2016, July 19). US election: Melania Trump "plagiarised" Michelle Obama. https://www.bbc.com/news/election-us-2016-36832095

Benoit, W. L., & Glantz, M. (2017). *Persuasive attack on Donald Trump in the 2016 Republican primaries*. Lexington Books.

Best New England Patriots Deflategate memes. (2021). *Liveabout*. https://www.liveabout.com/new-england-patriots-deflategate-memes-1923793

Dawkins, R. (1976). *The selfish gene*. Oxford University Press.

Deflategate. (2021). *Wikipedia*. https://en.wikipedia.org/wiki/Deflategate

Goldmacher, S., & Fandos, N. (2021, February 19). Ted Cruz's Cancún trip: Family texts detail his political blunder. *New York Times*. https://www.nytimes.com/2021/02/18/us/politics/ted-cruz-storm-cancun.html

Hafner, J. (2018, April 10). Judge finalizes $25 million Trump University settlement for students of "sham university." *USA Today*. https://www.usatoday.com/story/news/politics/onpolitics/2018/04/10/trump-university-settlement-judge-finalized/502387002/

Know Your Meme. (2021). The most interesting man in the world. https://knowyourmeme.com/memes/the-most-interesting-man-in-the-world

Kurtzman, D. (2020, January 13). Funniest Melania Trump memes. liveabout. https://www.liveabout.com/funniest-melania-trump-memes-4064562

Milner, R. M. (2016). *The world made meme*. The MIT Press.

Munson, O. (2022, October 13). What is a meme? They can be funny and cute or full of misinformation. We explain. *USA Today*. https://www.usatoday.com/story/news/2022/10/13/what-is-a-meme-definition-examples/8074548001/

Satija, N. (2019, June 5). Echoes of Biden's 1987 plagiarism scandal continue to reverberate. https://www.washingtonpost.com/investigations/echoes-of-bidens-1987-plagiarism-scandal-continue-to-reverberate/2019/06/05/dbaf3716-7292-11e9-9eb4-0828f5389013_story.html

Shifman, L. (2014). *Memes in digital culture*. MIT Press.

20 photos(hops) from Ted Cruz's Cancun vacation. *KnowYourMeme*. https://knowyourmeme.com/editorials/collections/20-photoshops-from-ted-cruzs-cancun-vacation.

Taylor, J. R., Stein, K. A., & Barton, M. H. (2023). Say it like you meme it: Looking back on Covid memes as an extension of the news cycle. *Northwest Journal of Communication, 50*(1), 59–110.

# · 2 ·

# CHARLIE SHEEN'S UNHINGED ATTACK ON PRODUCER CHUCK LORRE, CBS, AND WARNER BROS.

Is it better to be famous or infamous? If you are Charlie Sheen, the answer might be both. Sheen, a Golden Globe-winning, Emmy-nominated actor, starred in such high-profile films as *Wall Street*, *Major League*, *Hot Shots*, *Platoon*, *Young Guns*, and *Red Dawn*. He also had major roles in TV shows like *Two and Half Men*, *Spin City*, and *Anger Management*, along with cameos in *Friends*, *The Goldbergs*, *Big Bang Theory*, and *CSI*. In 2010, Sheen was the highest-paid actor on TV, making 1.8 million per episode (Bacardi & Mortellaro, 2017). Additionally, Sheen set a Guinness World Record for the fastest person on Twitter to reach a million followers (adding an average of 129,000 new followers per day) (Wasserman, 2011).

Surprisingly, *Two and a Half Men* went on hiatus in January 2011, while Sheen underwent a rehab program in his home, his third in 12 months. These issues, combined with derogatory comments aimed at award-winning producer Chuck Lorre (e.g., *Big Bang Theory*, *Roseanne*) and Warner Bros., got Sheen banned from the lot. Notwithstanding his status as the highest-paid actor on TV, Sheen demanded a 50% raise as part of his battle with Lorre and the studio. Apart from his acting achievements, his off-screen behavior garnered equal attention.

In 2015, Sheen announced he was HIV (human immunodeficiency virus) positive. This news, labeled the "Charlie Sheen effect," led to 1.25 million people googling the term HIV and gave the disease an important increase in public awareness. Despite this small silver lining of increased health exposure, Sheen's behavior was more accurately viewed as a natural consequence stemming from his reckless sex life (Spargo, 2015). Sheen was considered a womanizer—dating adult film actresses and engaging in criminal behavior such as domestic assault on his then-fiancé Kelly Preston (Derschowitz, 2011) and persistent drug abuse leading to numerous stints in rehab (Korba, 2015).

Ironically, through all of this turmoil, public perception was mixed. For example, in 2012, Fiat Motors used Sheen as its spokesman to promote their new Fiat 500 Abarth car (Pagliery, 2012). He also continued to garner on-screen work (e.g., *Scary Movie V* and the TV show *Anger Management*). Divergently, actor Corey Feldman accused Charlie Sheen of sexually abusing frequent co-star and friend, Corey Haim, during filming for the 1986 movie *Lucas* (Cordero, 2020). Amidst this public back-and-forth about the actor's past and present, Sheen could not choke back his feelings of injustice. His vitriol ramped up again in 2021 when he reflected on the 10-year anniversary of his "Tiger Blood" phase, a time where he gave several unhinged interviews (Heller, 2021).

This chapter examines Sheen's persuasive attacks on Chuck Lorre and Warner Bros. following his firing from *Two and a Half Men*. These attacks are found primarily in his *Good Morning America* interview, his appearance on the Alex Jones radio show, his "Sheen's Corner" live stream broadcast, and his open letter to Lorre.

## Attacks on Chuck Lorre, Warner Bros, and CBS

Sheen's attacks addressed two key topics: (1) Charlie Sheen is King and Chuck Lorre is less than human; and (2) CBS/Warner Bros. will lose a substantial amount of money as well as loyal viewers.

## Sheen vs. Lorre and CBS/Warner Bros.

Sheen combines attacks by suggesting that the only reason that *Two and Half Men* has been successful is his skill as an actor, not because Lorre can write or the network understands how to create award-winning programming. His rhetoric focused on two aspects of the character side of persuasive attack. First, by enhancing perceptions that the target possesses the trait (performed acts consistent with the trait and associating with others who share the trait), and second, by enhancing perceptions that the trait is particularly offensive.

## Accused Has Performed Acts Consistent with the Trait

In a TMZ interview, Sheen claims that Lorre's character is weak. He stated, "What does this say about Haim Levine [Chuck Lorre] after he tried to use his words to judge and attempt to degrade me. I gracefully ignored this folly for 177 shows ... I fire back once and this contaminated little maggot can't handle my power and can't handle the truth" (TMZ, 2011b). Here, Sheen suggests that Lorre is not only thin-skinned but that he has something to hide and is therefore justified in retaliating with a bigoted reference to Lorre's faith tradition. Moreover, Sheen furthers the attack in the Ustream interview by showing that not only is Lorre weak, he is in fact a coward. "Where ya hiding silly clown? Behind your narcissism? Your greed? Your hatred of yourself? Or women? Which personality are you cowering beneath for transparent cover. I see you, you little worm. I see you behind your plastic smile and your bitchy pout and your desperate need to be liked" (Ustream, 2011). Sheen clearly attempts to build a case condemning Lorre's character and further compounds this claim by calling up the show's (*Two & Half Men*) ratings without him. He asserted, "How's last night's 2.8 in the demo feel. Ouch. How about last night's 2.6 as well to follow it? Should have gone up. Instead it went down like you on some four dollar trollop" (Ustream, 2011). Sheen attempts to portray Lorre as a despicable person with questionable judgment as well as a failed producer, despite his achievements, which can only be explained by Sheen's acting prowess.

## Accused Associates with People Who Share the Trait

In his attack on Lorre and those involved in creating and those behind the scenes for *Two and Half Men*, Sheen explained that he is ready to get back to work, but he is hesitant to give anyone associated with the show a free pass on their behavior. He noted, "but if I bring up these turds, these little homunculean [sic] losers—there's just no reason to bring them back into the fold because I have real fame; they have nothing, they have zero" (TMZ, 2011a). Again, Sheen is clustering his enemies into a single category based on the same character trait he sees in Lorre—a veneer of fame contrasted with his own authentic success.

## Exemplify the Trait with a Particularly Offensive Example

Sheen attempts to solidify his characterization of Lorre and his former bosses by offering three specific examples to illustrate his contempt for them. First, he attacks Lorre and his battle with alcoholism:

> Think of me as you pray to the silly god of AA, while begging refuge from the contaminated image of hatred and dismay that so painfully glares back … Can you smell the imposter living within? Can you smell the whimpering scared child you'll never have the courage to embrace? Can you smell your mother's tears from some distant memory as she stared at her pathetic creation asking all around her why this feeble abortion survived? … You picked a fight with a warlock, you little worm. Remember this after that first drink back. The drink you know you want. The drink you can't avoid any longer. How's it taste? How's it feel? Are you whole again? At peace, in love? You are no match for this warlock (Ustream, 2011).

Not only does Sheen attack Lorre's resolve to improve his life via a widely accepted pathway, he taunts him to invoke a sense of how weak his commitment really is to stop drinking. In addition, he implies that even Lorre's own mother is sad that he survived, perhaps the ultimate attempt to malign his worth.

Sheen continues his tirade by expanding to others involved in the *Two and Half Men* work circle: "Number one, Les than Goonves [Les Goonves], part scoundrel, part … my hair to the side. Screw Les, I proclaim. Or better yet, screw more. You gave me your word so, in turn, you gave me nothing. It must really suck being your Mrs. The promise of getting something, yet receiving nothing … all shiny pool boys rejoice and line the block around your house. Sizzle losing. Bye" (Ustream, 2011). Here, Sheen attacks the then CBS chief executive officer (CEO), Goonves, for not only going back on his word but also failing as a man and a husband. He concludes his rant by showing the marked distinction between his success and their status as subhumans: "Canned slabs of jaundiced gorilla pelts fill the plates of those fools and clowns. Oh how they once begged to attend my perfect banquet in the nude. Now they just beg for the keys to my gold" (Ustream, 2011).

This strategy of using specific personal and grievous examples of behavior works to smear the reputation and undermine the credibility of any and all individuals involved. Sheen hopes that by using strong and judgmental language, his own behavior will seem more restrained than it might otherwise be.

## Financial Impacts and Fan Loyalty

The other part of Sheen's attack relates to the financial impact of other people's choices and how those decisions impact viewership. There are two factors Sheen combines to show how illogical and foolish it is for a network to engage in behaviors that directly affect their bottom line. He combines increasing perceived responsibility and increasing perceived offensiveness to make his case for undermining Lorre and other top-level executives.

### Increasing Perceived Responsibility

In the Good Morning America (GMA) interview, Sheen focuses on the huge financial misstep Warner Bros.TV made in terminating his contract by addressing questions related to his plans to pursue legal action. Host Savannah Guthrie asked Sheen about the estimated US$250 million the show lost following his departure. He responded, "It's going to cost them a lot more because they're on a battlefield and they let their emotions and their ego, um, basically they strapped on their diapers so, um, they're in breach. They're in radical breach and sorry guys, you screwed up" (Good Morning America, 2011). The implication of this attack is that Warner Bros. is not only in breach of contract, which is grounds for legal action, but the implication is that they were also being unethical and, by extension, untrustworthy.

### Increasing Perceived Offensiveness

Building on the ill will from the increasing perceived responsibility, Sheen adds to the offensiveness of his attack by making the extent of the damage more apparent. When asked what he intended to sue for during the GMA interview, he noted, "Tons. They're gonna actually put it on a scale and be like "a little more. A little more. Ah, add some gold. Add some gold. Oh your toupe is...bingo." (Good Morning America, 2011). Hyperbole aside, the implication is clear in that even if Sheen receives a large payout from a lawsuit, it won't be enough to make the situation right again.

To further his point about the scope of offensiveness, Sheen discusses the impact on the show's fans, who look to this outlet as a place of relaxation and entertainment: "I urge all my beautiful and loyal fans who embraced this show for almost a decade to walk with me side-by-side as we march up the steps of justice to right this unconscionable wrong" (TMZ, 2011). Sheen attempts to stoke a sense of public outrage for ruining the show, implying that the collective damage he has reported is accurate; otherwise, why would they fire the star of a successful show approaching its ninth season, a notable milestone for any network sitcom?

## Observations and Conclusions

Reaction to Sheen's attack discourse reveals some interesting findings. According to a Rasmussen Report poll taken in March 2011, only 16% of adults had a favorable opinion of the actor. Despite dominating news headlines, audience reactions varied from being very interested in the "dirty details" to disenchantment with a person who often presents himself in a staccato and chaotic fashion (Rice, 2011). Despite the unusual nature of Sheen's strategies, it appears that they serve two purposes. First, Sheen's attack performs a cathartic function for him: storing strong pent-up emotion, rational or not, is destructive to his future. Benoit (1999) argues in his functional theory of political campaign discourse that one of the primary purposes of an attack is to reduce another person's credibility so that it is lower than that of the person making the attack. In making his attacks, Charlie Sheen should be trying to lower Chuck Lorre's credibility along with others at CBS. He may very well have accomplished that, but his extreme behaviors also function to diminish his own credibility in an unanticipated zero-sum game. His cathartic outburst may make him feel better, but it is counterproductive to his intention of creating a contrast between his credibility and that of those he is attacking. Second, as Benoit (1995) notes in previous writing, attacking the accuser is a viable method to repair an image, meaning that whether the approach works or not, its use is still considered acceptable. Clearly, Sheen is not done with his career, but he needs to garner enough public good will to move forward with his aspirations as an actor.

There are three takeaways from examining the Sheen case. First, character attacks must use strong, uncommon, and highly personalized language to draw attention to the perceived injustice. However, they may fall short in terms of their actual impact precisely because they flirt with the line of the absurd. Second, logic must be present in the attacks to balance the use of strong and provocative emotional appeals. For instance, Sheen's choice to focus on financial loss is consistent with a society that judges success by monetary standards. Money is often used as a common justification for certain types of behavior, even when lined with greed (e.g., Sheen asking for a 50% salary increase when he was already TV's highest-paid actor). Third, people can distance themselves from the occasional bad choice but cannot distance themselves from their character with the same ease. Charlie Sheen's goal is to create a minefield for Chuck Lorre that is so packed with character booby traps as to render each public step hazardous. Consider public figures like Mel Gibson, Paula Dean, and Michael Richards, who all made statements considered racist, and even after apologizing for their behavior, people were slow to forgive because they believed these choices were driven by the core of each individual. As such, the hope for any change to the individual is highly unlikely. Ironically, Sheen may have done more damage to his own image than he did to Lorre by attacking him so unabashedly.

# References

Bacardi, F., & Mortellaro, A. (2017, March 23). Highest-paid TV casts of all time, by the numbers. *E-online*. https://www.eonline.com/news/838223/highest-paid-tv-casts-of-all-time-by-the-numbers

Benoit, W. L. (1995). *Accounts, excuses, apologies: A theory of image restoration strategies*. State University of New York Press.

Benoit, W. L. (1999). *Seeing spots: A functional analysis of presidential television advertisements, 1952–1956*. Praeger.

Cordero, R. (2020, March 10). Corey Feldman accuses Charlie Sheen of sexually abusing Corey Haim in (My) Truth documentary. *Entertainment Weekly*. https://ew.com/movies/corey-feldman-accuses-charlie-sheen-abuse-corey-haim-my-truth-documentary/

Derschowitz, J. (2011, May 4). Charlie Sheen: I didn't shoot Kelly Preston. *CBS News*. https://www.cbsnews.com/news/charlie-sheen-i-didnt-shoot-kelly-preston/

*Good Morning America*. (2011, March 11). Charlie Sheen interview. *YouTube*. https://www.youtube.com/watch?v=WViRdsBRKtM&t=1s

Heller, C. (2021, February 26). Charlie Sheen reflects on his regrets 10 years after "tiger blood" phase. *E Online*. https://www.eonline.com/news/1242194/charlie-sheen-reflects-on-his-regrets-10-years-after-tiger-blood-phase

Korba, A. (2015, November 16). Charlie Sheen: A timeline of a troubled life. *USA Today*. https://www.usatoday.com/story/life/people/2015/11/16/charlie-sheen-timeline-troubled-life/75893700/

Pagliery, J. (2012, March 2). Fiat is 'winning' with Charlie Sheen ad. *CNN Money*. https://money.cnn.com/2012/03/02/autos/charlie_sheen_fiat/index.htm

Rice, L. (2011, March 7). Poll: Charlie Sheen is not winning. *Entertainment Weekly*. https://ew.com/article/2011/03/07/poll-charlie-sheen-is-not-winning/

Spargo, C. (2015, November 18). Revealed: How Charlie Sheen spent over $1.6 million in a year on prostitutes while HIV-positive as famous madam says star paid extra to have sex without condoms - and favored 'pre-op transexuals'. *The Daily Mail*. https://www.dailymail.co.uk/news/article-3323670/How-Charlie-Sheen-spent-1-6million-YEAR-prostitutes-HIV-positive-famous-madam-says-star-paid-extra-sex-without-condoms-favored-pre-op-transsexuals.html

TMZ (2011a, February 24). Sheen RIPS 'Men' creator, AA and Thomas Jefferson. https://www.tmz.com/2011/02/24/charlie-sheen-two-and-a-half-men-chuck-lorre-argument-radio-talk-show-tirade-turd-thomas-jefferson/

TMZ (2011b, February 25). Charlie Sheen rages in open letter. https://www.tmz.com/2011/02/24/charlie-sheen-open-letter-two-and-a-half-men-chuck-lorre-tirade-turd-production-season-shut-down-crew-cbs-warner-bros/

Wasserman, T. (2011, March 3). Charlie Sheen sets new Guinness World Record for Twitter. *CNN*. http://edition.cnn.com/2011/TECH/social.media/03/03/charlie.sheen.twitter/index.html

Ustream (2011, March 8). Charlie Sheen - Sheen's Korner - Declares war on Warner CBS/ Chuck Lorre. https://www.youtube.com/watch?v=OVjglThBnD8

# · 3 ·

# "YOU MUST BE OUT OF YOUR DAMN MIND": ADAM LAROCHE AND THE SIN OF PUTTING FAMILY FIRST

In a world where the average professional baseball player makes over US$4 million a year (ESPN, 2021), it is hard to imagine why a successful player like Adam LaRoche would walk away from more than three times that amount—yet he did. His motivation for doing so was team president Ken Williams' criticism of LaRoche for bringing his son to work with him every day. Williams said directly to LaRoche:

> Listen, our focus, our interest, our desire this year is to make sure we give ourselves every opportunity to focus on a daily basis on getting better. All I'm asking you to do with regard to bringing your kid to the ballpark is dial it back. I don't think he should be here 100 percent of the time. And he has been here 100 percent, every day, in the clubhouse. I said that I don't even think he should be here 50 percent of the time. Figure it out, somewhere in between. ("Adam LaRoche retired," 2016)

LaRoche initially responded to Williams' request by tweeting a message, which included the hashtag #familyfirst: "Thank u Lord for the game of baseball and for giving me way more than I ever deserved! #familyfirst." Soon after, LaRoche announced his retirement from baseball and his leaving on the table a US$13 million contract. Surprisingly, the public response to his decision was cast in immoral language. For example, a Milwaukee Brewers pitcher argued: "I honestly think this is between good and evil. I know which side Adam lives on. I'm thankful to see the way he's acting […]." Then Washington Nationals All-Star outfielder Bryce Harper also expressed support: "Good for you Roche! Nothing like father and son in the clubhouse … It's a FAMILY game #FamilyFirst" (Bahr, 2016). In fact, LaRoche received so much support that even his White Sox teammates threatened to boycott an upcoming game against the Brewers in support of LaRoche's decision (Rapp, 2016). Eventually, the team did play, but not before a heated exchange took place in the locker room, where ace White Sox pitcher Chris Sale told Williams to "get out of the clubhouse and stay out" (Rapp, 2016).

ESPN sports analysts did not respond as favorably to the decision. Skip Bayless called LaRoche's desire to have his son around "excessive, bordering on obsessive" and suggested that he was "taking advantage of the privilege" of having his son in the locker room. Steven A. Smith agreed with Bayless' remarks, adding: "He [Williams] was absolutely right. There was not a speck of what he said that was wrong. I completely and wholeheartedly agree with him." Smith continued commenting on the White Sox players' decision to boycott a game by suggesting that "if Karl Ravech's report is true…and the Chicago White Sox are talking about boycotting the game, I want to stand here on national television and encourage the city of Chicago to boycott the White Sox because you must be out your damn mind." Although claiming he did not want to cast aspersions on Adam LaRoche, he still attacked his decision and anyone who would support it by saying "it's stupid, it's petty, and it's absolutely, positively ridiculous" (ESPN *First Take*, 2016).

In making sense of this public discussion, it is interesting that LaRoche's decision to walk away from baseball is considered a public offense rather than a personal decision as a father. In most cases of public scandal, people would account for behaviors that clearly harmed other people, such as infidelity, bigotry, abuse, and deception. In this case, however, a good and caring father is being attacked for putting family before money and his son before baseball.

This chapter will apply Benoit's persuasive attack framework to examine criticism levied toward LaRoche for his poor job decision-making and poor parenting. The analysis examines the ironic context of this attack on a public figure. There are four themes that reveal the nature of the attack against LaRoche and his decision to retire: (1) LaRoche's unreasonable request; (2) illogical financial decision; (3) inconsistent team leadership; and (4) weakening team chemistry.

## Attacks Surrounding LaRoche's Decision

LaRoche's decision, although seemingly personal, had a ripple effect in the way it impacted others. Attackers directed their comments primarily at LaRoche himself and Chicago White Sox Executive Vice President Kenny Williams.

## LaRoche's Unreasonable Request

These attacks reinforce the strategy of enhancing perceptions that the target possesses an undesirable trait and acts consistent with the trait. They begin by focusing on the unreasonable nature of LaRoche's request to bring his son to work with him every day. One article characterized the attack this way:

> You start here with Adam LaRoche, who decides to walk away from the White Sox and baseball ... because the White Sox won't allow him to take his 14-year-old son to work with him whenever he wants to. This action from LaRoche, no matter how sincere he is with his love for his son, and no matter how sincere he is wanting to have his son with him as much as possible, does not make him Rosa Parks. (Lupica, 2016)

What is interesting about this attack is the way in which a desired behavior (e.g., time together) is viewed as something distastefully manifest in LaRoche's decision and further minimized by comparing his reaction to a touchstone event in the struggle for civil rights. This same article continues the historical attack by noting:

> About this, though, there is no debate: Kenny Williams is not the bad guy here. And Adam LaRoche isn't a victim, or some kind of American hero. He doesn't refuse to sit in the back of the bus here. He makes a choice to get off it, acting as if the White Sox are somehow interfering with his right to be a good dad. They're not. (Lupica, 2019)

Clearly, the implication of this attack shows disdain for LaRoche's lack of ability to see that he is in a privileged position and that allowing all parents to bring their children to work would be impossible because the workplace is for adults and cannot function any other way.

A second attack on the unreasonable request focuses on the sacrifice other big leaguers are making, suggesting that LaRoche is not the only one giving up family time and, in some ways, has it better than many others. For example, Jose Abreu, who reported not seeing his son in three years, also references Alexei Ramirez, who missed time with his five children during the grueling

162 game major league season. The columnist concludes the list of examples noting, "there are players kicking and screaming that LaRoche might have had to take a few hours' break? Good lord, guys. Perspective. Please" (Snyder, 2016). This attack attempts to show that LaRoche is acting in a selfish manner and thereby inadvertently drawing negative attention to his own desires because, in essence, he is being told "no," you cannot bring your son to work.

A third attack on the unreasonable nature of LaRoche's decision involved the potential irreversible harm he may be inflicting on his son's emotional development. These attacks increased negative perceptions of the act and argued that LaRoche had a parental obligation to protect his son in all aspects of his life. For example, sports journalists attack LaRoche for his comment: "We're not big on school. He's going to learn a lot more useful information in the clubhouse than he will in the classroom" (Snyder, 2016). They respond very directly by suggesting LaRoche is limited in his vision and, even worse, shirking his paternal responsibility by limiting his son's age-appropriate opportunities. Michael Wilbon (2016), from ESPN's *Pardon the Interruption*, states:

> Nobody's kid needs to be in a professional locker room every day. It never should have happened in the first place … but here's the thing, Kenny Williams in his remarks … and other people from the White Sox says, we like this kid a lot, but we don't want anybody's kid, no kid ought to be in any workplace everyday. Go to school, then go to the library, then go to somewhere else kids go. You don't need to be in a professional environment of any kind, that includes my kid, everyday.

Additional attacks were even more to the point: "Adam LaRoche, meantime, is everyone's father of the year. For what? Enveloping his kid in some strange, alternate reality" (Madden, 2016). In short, LaRoche was heavily criticized for his position that he was benefiting his son with his unique socialization strategies.

## Financial Attack for Leaving Behind US$13 Million

The attacks against LaRoche also appealed to the pragmatic and highly controversial nature of athlete salaries. For instance, one columnist stated, "Adam LaRoche has made a killing playing ball, but he made a silly decision to cut his money trail short" (Cashman, 2016). Other attacks increased the gravity of his resolve to sever his ties with the MLB by noting the impact on the family he claims he is protecting. "If I were LaRoche's wife, I would let him sleep on the couch for at least a year. Who leaves a $13 million contract on the table because your boss says you can't bring your son to work every day? Hey, hubby, you're there to do your job, bring home the bacon and take care of your family. It's not the team's responsibility to provide daycare for our boy, that's our job" (Cashman, 2016). These attacks illustrate Benoit's strategy of increasing negative perceptions of the act by noting the extent of the damage.

## Inconsistent Account or Outright Lies from Williams

This set of attacks was concerned with the actual facts of the situation and how they might have changed, suggesting that the White Sox and their Executive Vice President (VP) Ken Williams in particular should be criticized as much or more than LaRoche. Part of this vitriol comes from accusations that Williams' decision to crack down on LaRoche did nothing more than hurt the team and weaken chemistry between players and between players and management. Jaffe (2016), writing for *Sports Illustrated*, noted:

> While Williams wasn't wrong when he asked rhetorically, "You tell me where in this country can you bring your child to work every day?" What makes very little sense at this juncture is why after calling Drake "a great young man," he went back on his previous agreement with LaRoche … a contract may have been violated; at the very least, the trust between Williams and LaRoche certainly was.

The concerns over inconsistency were perpetuated by White Sox pitcher Chris Sale, who argued during an interview that Williams lied to the team during a meeting with players, "… Williams told the players that coaches were complaining about Drake's presence. Then went to coaches and said players were complaining. Then held a clubhouse meeting and said chairman Jerry Reinsdorf was complaining" (Jaffe, 2016). Sale continued his attack during a different interview, where he responded to a reporter's question about whether Williams had created a new team policy: "Kenny said quite a few things, contradicting statements … he came to the players, said it was the coaches, went to the coaches, said it was the players and then came in here and told us it was the owners. We're not exactly sure who it was coming from, who it originated from … um … that's why we're still trying to figure out where it all came from"

(WGN Radio, 2016). Fellow White Sox teammate Todd Frazier, who joined the team in the offseason, commented: "I'm a big loyalty guy, a big promise guy ... If you're going to promise somebody something you have to go through with it, whatever that is, or to the extent to whatever it was" (Nightengale, 2016). In sum, these attacks all suggest that Williams' decision to confront LaRoche was hypocritical because he acquiesced to whatever audience he was addressing. When these audiences interacted, it was clear that they felt the inconsistency was indicative of an indecisive leader who should not be trusted on this issue.

## Weakening Team Chemistry

Not only did inconsistency cast doubt on Williams' credibility, but other attacks suggested his behavior directly weakened team chemistry. Such attacks showcase Benoit's strategy of increasing negative perceptions of the act by documenting the persistence of negative effects, an unintended consequence of certain statements or behaviors. Jaffe (2016) criticizes Williams' timing, implying that he should have addressed this issue before the start of spring training. He suggested that if LaRoche would have retired no matter when this issue was discussed, "the Sox might have used the US$13 million savings to sign Dexter Fowler or Ian Desmond or another free agent who could have provided a more substantial upgrade." Jaffe also reported that,

> Tensions have since increased. When Williams met with the team, Sale "absolutely lit up" the exec...the main thrust of Chris Sale's anger with Kenny Williams was that he's not around enough to understand the dynamics of the White Sox clubhouse and that it was Williams's unilateral overruling of Hahn and Ventura in such a context that set players off.

During his WGN Radio (2016) interview, Sale further attacked Williams for being blind to the real impact of his comments about the club's ultimate goal: "We were rollin'. We were having a great time. You guys have seen it. The drills were crisp, everything was clicking, and uh, it just took someone to throw a wrench in it." Clearly, these attacks exhibit the way a comment can be used to demonstrate the full magnitude of a response.

## Observations and Conclusions

There are several key takeaways from the Adam LaRoche case. Each underscores the tenuous nature of public attacks, even in unusual circumstances like this one. For instance, LaRoche created the talking points about the importance of family and that he could not be bought on his principles. Surprisingly, LaRoche had a difficult time defending them (e.g., rearing a child in a clubhouse instead of a schoolhouse), instead watching as his explanations turned into ammunition against him. Clearly, the LaRoche case is evidence that the flow of the attack does not always go in favor of the attacker, even when a situation appears to be housed in a virtuous context. In other words, how can a defense that you want to (1) spend more time with your child, (2) you will not be derailed by money, and (3) you hold no ill will toward your employer for telling you "no" actually backfire? In this case, that is precisely what happened. The examples in this chapter clearly point out a surface-level appreciation for his attempt, but a certain level of disdain for his naive belief that having no separation from children is entirely healthy. This case reveals the interrelated nature of an act and the character traits that spur the act (Benoit, 2017). Accusing LaRoche of doing something "dumb," however well intentioned, implies a naïveté of the world and calls into question his overall intelligence. Thus, when an act is publicly attacked, the agent's character is also impugned.

A second takeaway is the way money alters the lens through which we evaluate a person's decision-making. Historically, public opinion polls have clearly revealed that professional athletes are definitely overpaid (Dierkes, 2018; D'Errico, 2002). Despite this frustration, it is as if the fan base is saying you are already in a privileged position, garnering an unbelievable paycheck that many people could not achieve in a working lifetime, so do not insult us further by walking away from it. This vicarious jealousy underscores the frustration people have with athletes who make an exorbitant salary and then whine about it when everything does not go the way they want. This lack of patience was an Achilles heel LaRoche did not anticipate or even realize, but one his attackers exploited.

A third takeaway is that, despite the fact that this offense is totally different from other misdeeds, current public opinion suggests that fans are more likely to react in the most derisive ways to most criticisms against players (Kelner, 2017; Global Sports Development, 2014). Typically, athletes make mistakes like domestic violence (e.g., NFL star Ray Rice), taking performance-enhancing drugs (e.g., Olympic sprinter Marion Jones), extra-marital affairs (e.g., PGA golfer Tiger Woods), and other deviant practices society shuns. While LaRoche's offense is categorically different, the public still responded harshly with a knee-jerk reaction to his request and subsequent justification. The predisposition to respond negatively to athletes' failures may prove to be an effective attack strategy, especially in this case. Logically, LaRoche should be entitled to walk away and live his life the way he chooses; after all, his behavior is far from criminal. Yet, the fans and the media have a myopic view of athlete behavior and only view it through the lens of how that behavior impacts the sport. In this way, the attacks against LaRoche were effective in elevating the significance of his decision beyond its personal impact on him and his family.

The final takeaway from the LaRoche case is that the ripple effects of his decision permeate multiple, relevant audiences. These audiences include his own family, his teammates, team management, and White Sox fans. Thus, each of these audiences requires different messages to be satisfied with his explanation. The problem is that these audiences sometimes require opposite messaging. For instance, his family may view the decision as appropriate and altruistic, while the fans may view it as letting down the team. These diverse perceptions become more important when we consider the need for accuracy and specificity as evidenced by the attacks on VP Ken Williams, not to mention how such decisions impact the team and their potential to achieve their purpose—winning a World Series. In essence, these attacks show that LaRoche failed to think deeply enough about how his audiences might react. The implication here for understanding public attack is that audiences are not homogenous, nor are they passive, so when an attack is launched, it should not be treated as one-dimensional. Through this analysis, we scoured the Internet, looking at all directions of the attack. It appears that LaRoche is unaware of all the attacks being levied against him because he underestimated how many channels there are for disseminating facts and opinions about his decision. It seems that an active public, armed with the ability to both create and access more information about any person or situation, makes it easier to create a comprehensive public scandal. This holds true even in a situation like this one, where the actual charge is minimal compared to infidelity, sexual harassment, or racism.

# References

Adam LaRoche retired over White Sox's request to limit son in clubhouse (2016, March 17). *ESPN*. espn.go.com/mlb/story/_/id/14989265/adam-laroche-retired-chicago-white-sox-asked-dial-back-son-clubhouse

Bahr, C. (2016, March 16). Adam LaRoche retired because White Sox had issues with his son. *Fox Sports*. www.foxsports.com/mlb/story/adam-laroche-chicago-white-sox-retire-ken-williams-son-clubhouse-drake-family-031616

Benoit, W. L. (2017). Criticism of actions and character: Strategies for persuasive attack extended. *Relevant Rhetoric, 8*, 1–17.

Cashman, J. (2016, March 19). Adam LaRoche should have left the kid. *Boston Herald*. https://www.bostonherald.com/2016/03/19/cashman-adam-laroche-should-have-left-the-kid-at-home/

D'Errico, R. A. (2002, February 1). Poll finds New Yorkers think athletes overpaid. *Albany Business Review*. https://www.bizjournals.com/albany/stories/2002/01/28/daily50.html

Dierkes, T. (2018, February 7). Are MLB players overpaid? *MLB Trade Rumors*. https://www.mlbtraderumors.com/2018/02/mlb-players-overpaid.html

ESPN First Take (2016, March 17). Adam LaRoche puts family first in walking away from White Sox. https://www.youtube.com/watch?v=2ro5aydB2wQ

Global Sports Development (2014). Doping survey reveals public opinion. https://globalsportsdevelopment.org/doping-survey-reveals-public-opinion/

Jaffe, J. (2016, March 17). Bizarre Adam LaRoche controversy creating internal clash for White Sox. *Sports Illustrated*. https://www.si.com/mlb/2016/03/17/adam-laroche-chicago-white-sox-son-controversy

Kelner, M. (2017, July 4). General public is losing faith in scandal-ridden sports, survey claims. *The Guardian*. https://www.theguardian.com/sport/2017/jul/05/public-faith-sport-low-corruption-doping-sacndals-survey

Lupica, M. (2016, March 19). Adam LaRoche is no victim in rift with White Sox. *New York Daily News*. https://www.nydailynews.com/sports/baseball/lupica-adam-laroche-no-victim-riff-white-sox-article-1.2570765

Madden, M. (2016, March 18). Madden: Asking Adam LaRoche to cut back son's clubhouse time was not out of line. *The Times*. https://www.timesonline.com/article/20160318/Sports/303189989

Nightengale, B. (2016, March 18). In LaRoche-White Sox flap, Kenny Williams acted on behalf of others, too. *USA Today*. https://www.usatoday.com/story/sports/columnist/bob-nightengale/2016/03/18/adam-laroche-drake-laroche-kenny-williams/81993428/

Rapp, T. (2016, March 17). White Sox players reportedly considered boycott after Adam LaRoche retirement. *Bleacher Report*. bleacherreport.com/articles/2625496-white-sox-players-reportedly-considered-boycott-after-adam-laroche-retirement

Snyder, M. (2016, March 21). The five dumbest things about the White Sox-LaRoche saga. *CBS Sports*. https://www.cbssports.com/mlb/news/the-five-dumbest-things-about-the-white-sox-laroche-saga/

Wilbon, M. (2016, March 16). Wilbon: Nobody's kid needs to be in a locker room every day. *ESPN's Pardon the Interruption*. https://www.espn.co.uk/video/clip/_/id/14989625

WGN Radio (2016, March 21). Chris Sale: "This is us rebelling against B.S." https://www.youtube.com/watch?v=chA9QFAFRuY

# Part III
## POLITICAL ATTACKS

# · 4 ·

# REPUBLICAN SELFIE VIDEOS DENIGRATING DONALD TRUMP

This chapter conducts an exploratory analysis of persuasive attacks found in political selfie videos. As social media continues to flourish, selfies are becoming increasingly popular. In fact, some reports show that people spend 54 hours a year taking selfies, building up to a lifetime accumulation of 25,700 (Broz, 2022). Selfies cut across social media platforms from Facebook to Instagram and Snapchat to a host of image manipulation apps taking the form of photos or videos. For our purposes here, video selfies have become a medium for persuasive attacks.

On May 11, 2020, a group of eight Republicans (George Conway, Steve Schmidt, John Weaver, Rick Wilson, Jennifer Horn, Ron Steslow, Reed Galen, and Mike Madrid) established The Lincoln Project (2020), aka Republican Voters Against Trump (RVAT, 2020a–c). These messages attacked President Donald Trump repeatedly on a variety of grounds. Contempt for the GOP leader was evident in several of these messages. One video selfie, for example, declared, "I would vote for Howdy Doody, I would vote for Mr. Ed before I would vote for Donald Trump. In fact, I'd vote for a pile of my dog Snickers' poop from the backyard before I'd vote for Donald Trump" (Steve, GA). One voter characterized the president as "a 73-year-old man who is having national tantrums acting like a five-year-old child who didn't get the candy he wanted" (DG, NJ). Alluding to the *Andy Griffith Show*, Elaine from Georgia asserted, "I would vote for Barney Fife before I would vote for Donald Trump." Another voter said, "If they put a circus monkey up with a little hat, that's who would get my vote instead of Trump this time" (Thomas, NJ). Mazza (2020) reported that the group was "planning to spend $10 million promoting them across social media as well as on television, with some appearing on Fox News". Zengerle (2020) explained that "scrolling through the testimonials on RVAT's website, the message to Biden-curious Republicans is clear: You are not alone." People have made attacks via video selfies before, even criticizing political candidates. However, we believe this is the first time a group has encouraged submissions of video selfies attacking a presidential candidate and promoted those videos.

The RVAT webpage invited Republicans who were dissatisfied with President Trump to submit video selfies explaining their attitudes to others. The group's webpage offers to disseminate their stories to others:

> Thanks for letting us share your story! Try to keep your video to a couple minutes, look straight into the camera, and simply talk about things like this:
> Say your first name and where you live.
> Tell us the story of how your politics have changed in recent years.
> Did you vote for Trump in 2016? Why or why not?
> Who are you supporting in the 2020 presidential election? Why?

The webpage also provided advice for those who planned to make one of these videos:

> Your story is actually better when NOT scripted. Simply look at the camera – and start talking politics! If you make a mistake or stumble, that's perfectly fine. We may edit these videos for clarity and trim to an appropriate length, but we will keep your story intact. Have the light shining on your face, not behind you. (RVAT, 2020b)

So, RVAT invited Republicans to create and submit video selfies criticizing Republican President Donald Trump.

By mid-August, this group had attracted 104K subscribers and received over 30 million views (RVAT, 2020a). In addition to views racked up on the RVAT webpage, these video selfies have also been frequently viewed via social media such as Twitter and Facebook. Zengerle (2020) talked about one video from Josh in North Carolina:

"Hi, my name is Josh. I live in North Carolina, and I voted for Donald Trump," he begins, in a tone of abject resignation. He cocks his head and rolls his eyes. "My bad, fam," he apologizes. "Not my proudest moment. I will not be voting for him again." But since RVAT posted the video online, it has been viewed more than a million times on the group's Twitter account, seen more than 100,000 times on its YouTube channel and received plenty of media attention. (see also RVAT, 2020c)

This example establishes that these attacks on Donald Trump were disseminated widely; it is clear that other videos from this group were likely viewed widely as well.

Most of these videos included utterances that appeared to be intended to establish their credibility. Many selfies listed their connections to the Republican Party. Several of these Republicans stressed the length of their association with the GOP. For example, Chad from Missouri explained:

For as long as I can remember I've been a Republican. My parents and grandparents were staunch Republicans. I've always been very interested in conservative politics and considered myself a conservative for most of my life. In fact, when I was a teenager I read both of Rush Limbaugh's books, listened to his radio show, and programmed my VCR to record his TV show. [all voter quotations were transcribed from the RVAT webpage, rvat.org]

Robert, also from Missouri, told viewers that, "I have been a long-time Republican since Barry Goldwater in 1964 when I was age 13." We learned about Landsford's (NV) background: "I'm a lifelong Republican. My work with the party began back in the early '70s, I became finance chairman for the Republican Party in Northern Nevada." Similarly, Tom (also from Nevada) explained:

My loyalty to the Republican Party began at the age of 18 when I first registered to vote. Being from California I had the opportunity to work for former Governor Ronald Reagan ... I also served three years for a Republican congressman in Southern California. I also have total experience of about 20 campaigns – presidential, gubernatorial, senatorial, and congressional – for the Republican Party.

One voter told viewers that, "I was raised Republican in a Republican household. My parents were precinct officers, I served two terms in the North Carolina legislature as a Republican representative ... I served two terms as mayor" (Shawn, NC). Scott from North Carolina was a "lifetime Republican voter," while another speaker had been a "chapter chair of the College

Republicans" (Jonathan, NH). The point here is that these selfies are not from casual voters but from committed, long-term members of the GOP.

Other voters mentioned that they possessed other conservative credentials. Pat (MN) stated, "I was an evangelical pastor in Minnesota for 20 years." Dick (NM) said, "I'm a 71-year-old West Pointer and a former Army officer." Brian from New York declared that, "I spent 10 years active duty as a Navy Seabee [member of the Construction Battalion] and I'm still in the reserve." Scott (NC) was "an Army veteran, a former Army officer in the 82nd Airborne Division." Shawn is a "decorated Navy veteran" from North Carolina. Matt from Florida declared, "I worked in the Pentagon for the Joint Chiefs of Staff. I have written talking points for the National Security Council." Paula (NC) revealed that she "recently retired as a circuit court judge." In sum, pastors, former members of the Armed Services, judges, and police officers united to criticize the current Republican president.

This investigation of Republican video selfies against Donald Trump employs two methods. First, it undertakes an analysis of the functions and topics using Benoit's theory of the attacks in these messages (Benoit, 2007; 2014a,b). Second, it uncovers the strategies for intensifying attacks on behavior (policy) and character.

## Functional Analysis of Lincoln Project Video Selfies

The sample for this study consisted of 339 video selfies, at least one from each state. These texts were content-analyzed using the concept of attacks from the Functional Theory of Political Campaign Discourse (Benoit, 2007; 2014a,b).

Table 4.1 reports the results of the content analysis of these video selfies. They stressed character flaws (71%) far more often than they made policy complaints (29%). For example, Rob (TX) illustrated a character attack when he declared that Trump had committed the Seven Deadly Sins: gluttony, avarice, pride, sloth, anger, lust, and envy. He also said the president violated the Seven Cardinal Virtues: truth, love, courage, wisdom, tolerance, freedom, and creativity. Sins and virtues are elements of character. In addition, Cindy from Michigan criticized the target's character: Donald Trump is "a liar, bully, and amoral man." These videos also attacked President Trump's policies. His foreign policy was the subject of this attack: "Our standing in international politics has gone down the tubes with all the favors that Trump seems to do for Erdoğan, for Putin, for Kim Jong-un" (Dave, NV). Trump's domestic policy also comes under fire in a video selfie:

> The past three and a half years have been a disaster for Americans. We have an increasing federal debt that is currently seven times the annual revenue. We've got an unemployment rate not seen since the Great Depression. We've got the greatest racial and political divide not seen in at least 50 years. And we have the most devastating healthcare crisis in more than 100 years, killing, so far, more than 125,000 Americans. (Robert, FL)

This attack identifies several failed domestic policies during Trump's first term: federal debt, unemployment, the racial and political divide, and the coronavirus disease 2019 (COVID-19) pandemic. Statistical analysis revealed that the contrast in emphasis on policy and character was statistically significant ($X^2$ [$df$ =1]=445.1, $p<.0001$). We have no comparison data from other video selfies, but we can compare these results with data from attacks on the two candidates in the 2016 general presidential campaign ($X^2$ [$df$ =1]=360.44, $p<.0001$, $\varphi=.18$). The selfies stressed character in their attacks more than the two most recent presidential candidates (Benoit & Glantz, 2020). Inspection of Table 4.1 suggests that in other ways, these video selfies were generally similar to candidate discourse (past deeds were the most common form of policy and future plans the least common; personal qualities were the most common form of character and ideals the least frequent). Table 4.2 provides illustrative examples of these six forms of attack.

## The Theory of Persuasive Attack and Lincoln Project Video Selfies

The texts were examined using the strategies for enhancing persuasive attacks identified in the book's introduction (see also Benoit, 2017, 2020; Benoit & Glantz, 2020). The Theory of Persuasive Attack identifies the two components of a persuasive attack; responsibility (blame) and offensiveness, each of which is subdivided into several more specific strategies. It seems likely that these various strategies might not appeal equally to all people. Accordingly, it is possible that using a greater variety of strategies is a better strategic choice than using fewer strategies; hopefully some of the strategies will appeal to audience members. This section will illustrate strategies for intensifying attacks on actions and then attacks on character in Republican video selfies attacking President Trump.

Table 4.1. Functions of Attacks by Republican Voters Against Trump

| | Policy | | | Character | | |
|---|---|---|---|---|---|---|
| | Past Deeds | Future Plans | General Goals | Personal Qualities | Leadership Ability | Ideals |
| RVAT Selfies | 598 (77%) | 13 (2%) | 167 (21%) | 1313 (71%) | 296 (16%) | 253 (14%) |
| | | 778 (29% | | | 1862 (71%) | |
| 2016 Candidates | 2870 (71%) | 211 (5%) | 985 (24%) | 2963 (75%) | 630 (16%) | 364 (9%) |
| | | 4066 (51%) | | | 3957 (49%) | |

339 ads; candidate data from Benoit & Glantz (2020).

## Intensifying Attacks

Donald Trump was criticized for both domestic and foreign policy failures. The president's handling of the COVID-19 pandemic was one policy topic that came under fire in these video selfies. One voter refers to Vietnam, where "58,000 people died. And we've almost tripled that right now" (Jeffrey, TX). This attack stressed the extent of his failings. Amid the protests following George Floyd's death, President Trump went to St. John's Church in Lafayette Square for a photo op. "He walked down the street from the White House and held up a Bible in front of a church, a Bible he's probably never opened, in front of a church I'm sure he's never gone to. Gassing peaceful protesters" (Robert, NE). This passage stresses his hypocrisy (inconsistency) for using a Bible he allegedly never read and staging his photo op at a church he allegedly never attended. Gassing peaceful protesters suggests that his victims did not deserve to be tear gassed.

Trump's foreign policy also came under fire. Robert from New Hampshire charged that the president "has severely damaged our relationships with long-standing allies and tarnished our standing in the world." He was accused not of causing minor damage but of causing "severe" damage. Brian from New

York indicated that Trump knew "what Putin was doing, what Russia was doing" with bounties on US soldiers. He was aware of the bounties; he has no excuse for not taking action. Ridge from South Carolina implied that the President had an obligation to protect the victims of Russian bounties. "I've watched him refuse to approach Russia over paid bounties on US troops. That's unacceptable to me and it should be unacceptable to all Americans. Our service members are a very important part of our country and it's our job to elect leaders that make good choices on their behalf and on our behalf as well." Brian from Connecticut argued, "He puts his personal interests above the interests of the average American citizen every day," indicating that he benefited from his offensive acts. Jim from Maryland said we do not just have a bad president, but "the worst president... in the history of the United States," again intensifying the attack with extensiveness.

These videos also addressed President Trump's character. Pejan (IL) criticized his mental ability: "Trump simply does not have what it takes upstairs to perform the duties required to be a good president." Another voter declared that, "He's 100% unqualified for the job" (Bart, CO), stressing the extent of his incompetence. This comment attacks the president's cognitive faculties, suggesting that his brain power is minimal, a form of extent. John from New York points out that, "He's just done worse and worse things. The assault on the Gold Star family, their son fought for the United States and he died and should be held in the highest esteem and yet Trump totally disrespected these parents. He's done other things against John McCain, he's done things against our intelligence committee, he believes Vladimir Putin before he believes our intelligence committees." This passage stresses the extent of his disrespect. Donald Trump was criticized for repeated offenses: "He got five deferments from the draft ... four student deferments; however, when his student deferments ran out, suddenly he developed bone spurs, which miraculously cleared up as soon as the last helicopter left the American Embassy roof in 1975.... He's had over 25 different women make allegations of sexual misconduct against him. He has settled suits and signed non-disclosure agreements with porn stars he's had relationships with during each of his three marriages" (Ron, FL). Kim (IN) echoed the theme of repeated offenses when he declared that Trump is "a liar, a serial liar."

We want to mention one observation about emphasizing a problem through the strategy of extent. Obviously, the size of a problem can be indicated using numbers. Ian (IA) reported, "Donald Trump would sacrifice 140,000+ people" to the coronavirus pandemic." Another argument emphasizing the extent of

**Table 4.2.** Examples of Attacks on the Forms of Policy and Forms of Character in RVAT

| Policy | |
|---|---|
| Past Deeds | "Under President Trump's Administration and the new tax laws, I'm currently paying more in taxes as is everybody I know. The new tax laws solely benefitted corporations" (Debbie, NJ). |
| | "He has not spoken up about the possible bounties on the heads of our soldiers" (Caryn, NC). |
| | "He's destroyed our credibility globally, he's instigated pointless trade wars, and he's racked up huge deficits" (Joel, MA). |
| | "Our president told us that he would make this country first in the world. And that he did: He did make us first in infections in the world. He made us first in deaths in the world. And he made us first in economic disaster in this world" (Richard, NH). |
| | "Racial tensions, disease, unemployment … every negative thing we could possibly have in this country is current here right now" (DG, NJ). |
| Future Plans | "The man had no plan to govern, he had no plan for domestic policy, he had no plan for foreign policy" (Bob, FL). |
| | "There's no plan" for handling Covid-19 (Skip, NJ). |
| | "This idiot wants to put children in classrooms without having any plan" (Jeffrey, TX). |
| | "Didn't Trump say over and over again that he was creating this beautiful health care program, much better than Obamacare. Anyone hear of Trumpcare? I don't think so" (Steve, TX). |
| | "President Trump lacks an adequate plan on how to open up our country" (Debbie, NJ). |

*Table 4.2. Continued*

| Policy | |
|---|---|
| General Goals | "The man wants to destroy democracy and take over and be a dictator" (Roger, MA). |
| | By promoting reopening schools, he is "putting my children at risk going to school, the teachers putting them at risk" (Jeffrey, MA). |
| | "He was not looking to heal and unite, he was dividing" (Eric, CA). |
| | "I don't trust our healthcare system in this country under Donald Trump ... I don't trust what he would do with Medicare. I don't trust what he would do with Social Security benefits. I don't trust him with the country. I don't trust him with our military. I don't trust him, period, with anything" (Richard, GA). |
| | "Unlike Trump, however, I oppose favoring corporations based on their political relationship with the president" (Charles, HI). |
| **Character** | |
| Personal Qualities | "He lies. He lies about everything" (Dan, ID). |
| | "He's mean, he's vindictive, he acts like a two-year-old" (Carol, MN). |
| | "His serial lies, his overt racism, his corruption, his bullying, his misogyny" (Kim, IN). |
| | Trump is a "child, dangerous child" (David, MA). |
| | Donald Trump is an "obviously venal and crass person" (Matthew, MI). |
| | Trump "is just a small person ... just a rich, spoiled, little insecure brat" (Matt, CA). |

*Continued*

Table 4.2. *Continued*

| Policy | |
|---|---|
| Leadership Ability | "This guy couldn't lead his way out of a paper bag" (Jeffrey, Massachusetts). |
| | "There's no room for competence in Trumpism" (Ian, Iowa). |
| | "He's incompetent (Carol, Minnesota). |
| | "He is so unqualified" (Loretta, Minnesota). |
| | "Donald Trump is totally unfit for office" (Joel, Massachusetts). "He gave himself a 10 for 10 on how he's handling the coronavirus situation, which to me would be a joke if it were funny, but it isn't" (Jim, FL). |
| Ideals | Donald Trump is "an immoral person" (Mark, Maine). |
| | Donald Trump is "morally corrupt" (Joy, Missouri). |
| | "There is nothing conservative about" Trump (Naomi, Maryland). |
| | "President Trump has no morals" (Aaron, Nebraska). |
| | "He's undermining our most cherished values" (Matthew, New Jersey). |

Trump's foreign policy includes the impact of tariffs. For example, Lee (MD) declared, "We had to pay US$50 million in kickbacks to American farmers after Trump's trade wars to get our products sold abroad." However, the magnitude of a problem can also be emphasized in other ways. "The last four years have been a total train wreck" (Peter, MI). "Trump is a disaster for the country," added Fred (CT). The president "has racked up record deficits" (Michael, MI), emphasizing the size of this problem without using numbers. One voter said that "Donald Trump is so dangerous to our United States it's horrifying" (Phillip, CA). On his character, Kevin (AZ) asserted that Trump peddled a "multitude of lies," while Jill (DE) said he "has zero leadership." Karen (CA) stated, "He truly does not know what he's talking about," while Alejandro (FL) added, "I think he's the worst of humanity". Shelley (FL) concluded, "He has absolutely corrupted the presidency." The video from John (IL) claimed that "Trump is a bully, an unrelenting bully … His lies are legendary and unabashed … His ego is boundless." The terms "unrelenting," "legendary," "unabashed," and "boundless" all stress the huge magnitude of these defects.

We also collected data on the frequency of these strategies for intensifying persuasive attacks in these video selfies. As Table 4.3 shows, more of these strategies were found on behavior or policy (61%) than on character (39%; $\chi^2$ [$df$ =1]=15.51, $p<.0001$). Both groups of strategies have two components, one related to beliefs (blame, possessing trait) and one related to values (offensiveness). Curiously, the data show a sharp contrast between these two groups of strategies. In attacks on behavior, blame accounts for 62 instances and offensiveness for 126; in attacks on character, the existence of the trait comprises 115 examples, whereas offensiveness accounts for only 4 instances. This contrast was statistically significant with a very large effect size ($\chi^2$ [$df$=1]=15.51, $p<.0001$). $\chi^2$ [$df$=1]=120.96, $p<.0001$, $\varphi$=.63).

Table 4.4 offers several examples of the attack strategies used in video selfies. Interestingly, some utterances employ more than one strategy.

## Observations and Conclusions

The American public has become increasingly polarized (Pew Research Center, 2022). Going back a few years, Abramowitz and Webster (2016) reported, "A growing proportion of Americans dislike the opposing party more than they like their own party" (p. 21). This divide is reflected in attitudes toward President Donald Trump. In July of 2020, Trump's approval among Republicans edged up from 85% to 91%; the president's approval among Democrats dipped from 5% to 2% (Jones, 2020). A gap in the approval rating between Democrats and Republicans of 89% illustrates the extreme polarization in the United States.

Given the magnitude of the political divide in America in 2020, it would be unreasonable to expect that any message, for or against Donald Trump, would persuade all (or even most) voters. However, an estimated 10% of voters were undecided in August 2020, constituting about 21 million people (Jarvis, 2020). The number of individuals who might be persuaded to vote against President Trump was limited. Furthermore, only those people who watched

**Table 4.3.** Strategies for Intensifying Attacks in RVAT Videos

| Intensifying Attacks on Actions | |
|---|---|
| *Perceived Responsibility for Act* | |
| Committed the Act Repeatedly | 18 |
| Planned the Act | 2 |
| Knew Consequences (or Knew about Problem) | 9 |
| Benefitted from Act | 32 |
| Others Do Not Commit this Act | 1 |
| Act Seems Directed Toward Victim | 0 |
| Subtotal | 62 |
| *Negative Perceptions of Act* | |
| Extent of Harms | 80 |
| Persistence of Effects | 8 |
| Effects on Victims | 8 |
| Inconsistency | 3 |
| Victims of Acts | 21 |
| Obligation to Protect Victims | 6 |
| Subtotal | 126 |
| Total Attacks on Behavior | 188 (61%) |
| **Intensifying Attacks on Character** | |
| *Target Possesses Trait* | |
| Extent of Trait | 45 |
| Performed Acts Consistent with Trait | 4 |
| Made Statements Consistent with Trait | 16 |
| Associates with Unsavory People | 20 |
| Accused Contrasted with Respected People | 30 |
| Subtotal | 115 (39%) |
| *Trait is Offensive* | |
| Particularly Repulsive Example of Trait | 1 |
| People Negatively Affected by Trait | 3 |
| Subtotal | 4 |
| Total Attacks on Character | 119 |

**Table 4.4.** Examples of Strategies for Intensifying Attacks in RVAT Videos

| Intensifying Attacks on Actions | |
|---|---|
| *Perceived Responsibility for Act* | |
| Committed the Act Repeatedly | Trump has made "repeated attempts to destroy the American Constitution" (Don, NV). |
| | "He had gone bankrupt multiple times" (Loretta, MI). "This man dodged the draft five times" (Phillip, CA). |
| | "He's had over 25 different women make allegations of sexual misconduct against him … He's had relationships with [porn stars] during each of his three marriages" (Ron, FL). |
| | "You can't deny, deny, deny and then lie, lie, lie, lie" (Dawn, CO). |
| | "Donald Trump has demonstrated over and over again to be incompetent, to lack humility, to not take responsibility for his actions" (Kyle, KY). |
| Planned the Act | "He has been willfully ignorant and duplicitous and sociopathic, which is now to this date cost 140,000 and up deaths" (James, NY). |
| | After listing several ideals or values such as liberty, rule of law, fair and free elections, freedom of speech and assembly, separation of powers with checks balances, freedom of the press, one voter said "I cannot support a president who is systematically dismantling all that I have mentioned" (Leroy, UT). |

*Continued*

*Table 4.4. Continued*

| Intensifying Attacks on Actions | |
|---|---|
| Knew Consequences (or About Problem) | "He essentially ignored his public health experts for months. He ignored intelligence agencies telling him that this is serious and unfortunately many more people died that should have died. So many of these deaths could have been prevented" (Chris, FL). |
| | "He was warned about the dangers and the risks of the pandemic and he called it a hoax" (DG, NJ). |
| | "The fact that a president would stand by, knowingly (he's been briefed), he's know about this [Russian bounties on American soldiers] and has taken zero steps to rectify this situation" (Christopher, IA). |
| | "He didn't stop the pandemic. He knew from his briefings in January … that he should have started something immediately. And we would have saved thousands of lives" (Cheryl, IN). |
| | "He ignored warnings about the pandemic" (Bob, FL). |
| Benefitted from Act | "He's willing to do anything to anybody as long as it benefits him personally" (Roy, CA). |
| | "He's leaving our elections vulnerable to foreign interference because it benefits him" (Nicholas, NY). |
| | "It's just shocking to see the extent to which the Office of the President has been used, the power of the president has been used for personal gain" (Jonathan, NH). |

*Table 4.4. Continued*

| Intensifying Attacks on Actions | |
|---|---|
| | Trump "is a man who cares only about himself and advances his personal goals at the expense of the American people" (Marsha, IL). |
| | "Placing his daughter and son-in-law in charge of projects that are critical to the health and wellbeing of American citizens demonstrates that Donald Trump puts his own interests ahead of the interests of his country" (Barb, MI). |
| Others Do Not Do This | "You can't even have a conversation based on facts. It always goes back to these like infantile comments like fake news and all that. Who does that?" (Alberto, NC). |
| Act Seems Directed Toward Victim | No examples present. |
| *Negative Perceptions of Act* | |
| Extent of Harms | "Donald Trump has given us the 1918 pandemic, the 1928 Great Depression, and the 1968 race riots all in one" (Ronald, CA). |
| | "Placing trust in President Xi is one of the greatest acts of presidential incompetence in history" (Matthew, NJ). |
| | "President Trump has given us the biggest deficits in US history and the biggest debt in US history … with 40 million filing for unemployment, and over 100,000 dead" (Matthew, NJ). |

*Continued*

*Table 4.4. Continued*

| Intensifying Attacks on Actions | |
|---|---|
| | "Think back to 2016, he ran on 'drain the swamp.' He is the swamp! He's worst than the swamp. He is the scum at the bottom of the swamp" (Kelly, FL). |
| | "What's he done for us? Has he done anything for health care? Nope. He's been in office three and a half years, nothing for healthcare. Has he done anything for prescription drugs? Nope. Has he done anything to help the elderly out for medications and assistance and everything else? Nope. Has he done anything for infrastructure? Nope" (Tim, GA).<br>"Across the board Trump has been a catastrophic failure" (Frank, NY). |
| Persistence of Effects | "Donald Trump has done irreparable harm to this country" (Michael, ME). |
| | "He has set back the rule of law for decades" (Brandon, KS). |
| | "If he is given another four years our democracy and our system of checks and balances will be damaged beyond repair (Jan, MI). |
| | "The treatment of immigrant children under the Trump Administration will be a stain on our country forever … Those children will be traumatized to an extent that's probably impossible to be corrected and it is embarrassing to me that our country treated little children in such an inhumane way" (Paula, NC). |
| | "He's already caused so much damage that it's going to take years to recover" (Ed, NJ). |

*Table 4.4. Continued*

| Intensifying Attacks on Actions | |
|---|---|
| Effects on Audience/ Victims | "I'm retired with medical problems and don't trust our healthcare system in this country under Donald Trump. I do receive Medicare with my retirement and I don't trust what he would do with Medicare. I don't trust what he would do with Social Security benefits. I don't trust him the country, don't trust him with our military. I don't trust him, period, with anything. If you care anything about this country, about the future, which I do, I have grandchildren and I'm concerned about them and my children" (Richard, GA) |
| | "Donald Trump would sacrifice 140,000+ people and he would sacrifice our kids' health and our kids' families' health" (Ian, IA). Trump "is putting all of our families' lives at risk" (Lynn, MO). |
| | "My son comes to me last night and says: 'I can't hug my grandfather because I have to stay six feet away from him. And I may never get to hug him again" (Jessica, GA). |
| | "There is no way I can explain to my grandchildren that Donald Trump's behavior is acceptable for any person, never mind the President of the United States … I can't hope to leave a better country for my grandchildren with such as person as the President of the United States" (Jay, NC). |
| | "Bullying and prejudice in our public life sets a national tone, … compromises the moral education of our children" (Charles, HI). |

*Continued*

*Table 4.4. Continued*

| Intensifying Attacks on Actions | |
|---|---|
| Inconsistency | "Not only does he lie but if he says something that I know I've heard, he says he didn't say it" (Helen, CO). |
| | "Seven close associates have been convicted of crimes... five communication directors, four chiefs of staff... What happened to 'I know the best people'?" (Jim, CT). |
| | "Draining the swamp? He did. And then he refilled it with his own people, many of whom are in jail or will be in jail" (Dan, CT). |
| Obligation to Protect Victims | "Putin paying somebody in Afghanistan to kill our soldiers? That man is sworn to protect and serve" (Jose, FL). |
| | "I think he's failed in the most basic responsibility of the president, that being to protect the lives of American citizens" (Gary, RI). |
| | Donald Trump "steals money from military families for his vanity projects" (Mark, MI). |
| | "Donald Trump steals millions of dollars from the American public every time he goes to his own golf course on his own property to play golf" (Jenny, IN). |
| **Intensifying Attacks on Character** | |
| *Target Possesses Trait* | |
| Extent of Trait | "Donald Trump lies. He lies on a daily basis, if not on an hourly basis" (Jenny, IN). |

*Table 4.4. Continued*

| Intensifying Attacks on Actions | |
|---|---|
| | He "unquestionably has zero diplomacy, zero humanity, and is essentially probably not even human. He's a monster, he's horrible" (Daniel, FL). |
| | "His hatred of foreigners, his racial bias, his ignorance about basic facts of science and engineering is astounding" (Steve, NC). |
| | "This man dodged the draft five times. Seeing him speak to cadets at West Point is like inviting a pedophile to be a clown at a child's birthday party" (Phillip, CA). Donald Trump is "an extremely ruthless and immoral person" (Mark, ME). |
| | "He's 100% unqualified for the job" (Bart, CO). |
| | Everything "changed when a Category 5 hurricane called Donald Trump came roaring through" (Ryan, FL). |
| Acts Consistent with Trait | "He is a racist … he's a xenophobe … He has continued his politics of hatred and division, he has continued to cater to the racist and xenophobic elements of society" (Bob, FL). |
| | Trump was accused of an inadequate response to the coronavirus pandemic. "He has dismissed the Pandemic Response Team" (Bob, FL). |
| | "He cozies up to dictators, authoritarians, tyrants, despots, and he disrespects our allies" (Mark, AZ). |
| | "Placing trust in President Xi is one of the greatest acts of presidential incompetence in history" (Steve, NC). |

*Continued*

*Table 4.4. Continued*

| Intensifying Attacks on Actions | |
|---|---|
| Statements Consistent with Trait | "I am so disturbed by Trump's repeated callousness to the select few of our citizens who volunteered to defend our nation with their lives, for ridiculing John McCain's service as a POW in Vietnam, to trivializing the grief of Gold Star mothers who lost their children in the service of our country" (Charles, HI). |
| | "Trump's rhetoric just kept getting worse … the discriminating, putting down women and people and name-calling" (Eric, CA). |
| | "A person who has called our FBI scum, who has denigrated POWs, decorated combat war heroes, Gold Star families" (Dan, AZ). |
| | Trump was accused of being an incompetent leader. "He told us it was a hoax, told us it would go away. He has promoted nonsense cures" (Bob, FL). |
| | "Are you okay with Donald Trump not being a doctor, suggesting that we inject disinfectants? That we inject UC light into our body?" (Paul, CA). |
| Associates with Unsavory People | "Trump is as clueless and inept as Herbert Hoover and as vindictive as Richard Nixon" (Gregory, NC). "George Wallace would be proud and Bull Connor, who once had John Lewis beaten along with other Civil Rights activists when he was a sheriff in Alabama would be proud of Trump" (Bill, OH). |

*Table 4.4. Continued*

| Intensifying Attacks on Actions | |
|---|---|
| | "He openly admires dictators like Vladimir Putin and Xi Jinping" (Harvey, NY). |
| | "He has surrounded himself with corruption" (Mack, FL). |
| | "This president has numerous convicted felons in his inner circle" (David, CA). |
| | "He is a diehard Putin puppet" (Paul, NC). |
| Contrasted with Respected People | President Reagan "did not feel the need to demonize his political rivals. He never called Americans names, he never called the free press enemies of the people" (Shawn, NC). |
| | "I do not believe that the current president shares Lincoln's views on equality" (Donna, IN). |
| | He does not represent "the Republican Party of Lincoln, of Teddy Roosevelt, of Eisenhower (a Kansas native son), of Ronald Reagan and George H. W. Bush" (Brandon, KS). |
| | "Nixon's [failings and missteps] were very, very serious and very real. No question about it. But in my mind they pale in comparison to the problems on Donald Trump" (Doug, CA). "What he's doing right now is exactly what George Washington fought a revolution for" (Ryan, FL). |
| *Trait is Offensive* | |
| Particularly Repulsive Example of Trait | "Republicans don't put children in cages" (Shawn, NC). |

*Continued*

*Table 4.4. Continued*

| Intensifying Attacks on Actions | |
|---|---|
| People Negatively Affected by Trait | "His tariffs destroyed my aunt's small business. China didn't pay for those tariffs, our small businesses paid for those tariffs" (Kevin, NY). |
| | "What he's done to the children at the border is unconscionable. The damage, the horrific abuse of those precious children who are innocent. They've done nothing wrong" (Tiana, SC). "There are 130,000 Americans that no longer get to see tomorrow's sunrise because of this abysmal mismanagement of the coronavirus" (Robbie, AZ). |

these videos (or heard about them from friends, family, or coworkers) could be affected by these messages. As indicated above, millions have watched these videos, although surely not all viewers were undecided. Still, these viewers could represent a large enough number to reduce votes for Donald Trump in November.

These videos are generally well-conceived. This conclusion arises from several considerations. Given the fact that these selfies were made by voters, it is not surprising that they addressed concerns common to many people. These messages criticized his character and his policies. These attacks were sharpened using a variety of strategies for intensifying persuasive attacks (keep in mind that it is unlikely many people watched all of these messages, but because they were replete with intensifying strategies, many viewers probably were exposed to such strategies). Finally, these selfies were from people who did not seem to be "radical liberal socialists": These messages were from Republicans, some of whom had supported the GOP for years, some of whom had served the GOP, and some of whom had been in the armed forces or law enforcement. We evaluate these messages as generally persuasive in attacking his credibility, and their impact needs to be evaluated on the basis of whether or not they inflicted significant harm and not on whether they persuaded all voters to change their attitudes about Trump.

Another takeaway from this chapter is that these messages focused on both behavior (policy) and character. A wide variety of strategies were put to use in these attacks: six of six strategies for enhancing the offensiveness of an act and five of six strategies for assigning blame for an act; two of two strategies for intensifying the offensiveness of a trait; and five of five strategies for establishing that the target possessed the trait. In most contexts, attackers will select a handful of strategies, recognizing that not all strategies are appropriate given the circumstances or situation. In this case, those creating selfies felt that utilizing every strategy available to them was in their best interest. In political attacks, politicians are particularly vulnerable to both character and behavioral attacks because of their widespread connections to voters and other candidates, as well as their histories in office integrating platforms and enacting policies.

The fact that these videos were created by Republicans who were attacking the Republican president plays into the idea of reluctant testimony (Benoit & Kennedy, 1999). Messages from sources who are presumed to speak against their own self-interests, such as a Republican attacking another Republican, can be more persuasive than other messages because they take out one of the perceived motivations for attacking another candidate, which is extreme party loyalty. Anti-Trump selfies from Democrats could be dismissed easier than anti-Trump selfies from members of the GOP. This does not mean that Republicans will unquestionably accept messages from other Republicans, but such messages do have a certain cachet.

This study categorizes attacks on Trump into the topics of policy and character (each topic has three subforms). Numerous examples of attacks on the three forms of policy and character are reported. Unlike other messages from the 2016 campaign, these videos stressed character more frequently than policy. More of the strategies in these videos concern attacks on behavior than policy. Interestingly, values were stressed more often than beliefs when discussing attacks on behavior, but beliefs were emphasized more when discussing attacks on character. Attacks on immoral behavior ought to be more compelling than attacks on immoral attitudes or values.

It may be premature to apply these findings to other attacks because an attack is prompted, at least in large part, by the target under examination. These attacks are all aimed at a single person, President Donald Trump, and he may be (and, arguably, is) quite different from other potential targets of attack. To the extent that President Donald Trump is not and does not behave like other politicians, generalizing from these findings is perilous, but it does teach us something about how attack functions in this unique political context.

# References

Abramowitz, A. I., & Webster, S. W. (2016). The rise of negative partisanship and the nationalization of US elections in the 21st century. *Electoral Studies, 41*, 12–22.

Benoit, W. L. (2007). *Communication in political campaigns.* Peter Lang.

Benoit, W. L. (2014a). *A functional analysis of political television advertisements* (2nd ed.). Lexington Books.

Benoit, W. L. (2014b). *Political election debates: Informing voters about policy and character.* Lexington Books.

Benoit, W. L. (2017). Criticism of actions and character: Strategies for persuasive attack extended. *Relevant Rhetoric, 8,* 1–17. http://relevantrhetoric.com/CriticismofActionsa ndCharacter.pdf

Benoit, W. L. (2020). Character assassination and persuasive attack on CBS's *Face the Nation.* In S. A. Samoilenko, M. Icks, J. Keohane, & E. Shiraev, E. (Eds.), *Routledge handbook of character assassination and reputation management* (pp. 295–306). Routledge.

Benoit, W. L., & Glantz, M. (2020). *Presidential campaigns in the age of social media: Clinton and Trump.* Peter Lang.

Benoit, W. L., & Kennedy, K. A. (1999). On reluctant testimony. *Communication Quarterly, 47,* 367–387.

Broz, M. (2022, July 19). 28 selfie statistics, demographics, & fun facts. https://phototutorial.com/ selfie-statistics/

Jarvis, J. (2020, August 24). Undecided voters were key to Trump's win in 2016. Will they deliver again? *Newsweek.* https://www.newsweek.com/2020/09/04/undecided-voters-were-key-trumps-win-2016-will-they-deliver-again-1526824.html

Jones, J. M. (2020, July 6). Trump's job approval rating steady at lower level. *Gallup.* https:// news.gallup.com/poll/313454/trump-job-approval-rating-steady-lower-level.aspx

Mazza, E. (2020, May 29). Rank-and-file Republicans turn on Trump in new effort to block his reelection. *Huffington Post.* https://www.huffpost.com/entry/republican-voters-against-trump_n_5ed09e83c5b6aeca900f0949

Pew Research Center (2022, August 9). As partisan hostility grows, signs of frustration with the two-party system. https://www.pewresearch.org/politics/2022/08/09/as-partisan-hostil ity-grows-signs-of-frustration-with-the-two-party-system/.

Republican voters against Trump. (2020a). rvat.org

Republican voters against Trump. (2020b). Tell your story. rvat.org

Republican Voters Against Trump. (2020c, August 12). Youtube channel. *Youtube.com.* https:// www.youtube.com/channel/UC03-Q9vq-JyiStTnqasADVg

The Lincoln Project. (2020). *Wikipedia.* https://en.wikipedia.org/wiki/The_Lincoln_Project

Zengerle, J. (2020, August 5). These Republicans have a confession: They're not voting for Trump again. *New York Times Magazine*. https://www.nytimes.com/2020/08/05/magazine/republicans-confess-against-trump.html

# PERSUASIVE ATTACKS FROM 2020 GOP POLITICAL ACTION COMMITTEES

Political Action Committees (PACs), super PACs, and 527 groups (named for a provision in the US Tax Code that grants tax-exempt status to these groups) are organizations that accept donations and create and broadcast political election TV spots. Some of these groups send direct mail advertising to voters and engage in other activities. Today, such groups also post advertisements on YouTube and distribute them via social media. Research shows that spots from such groups attack more frequently than ads sponsored by candidates (Benoit, 2014).

Candidates probably hope that backlash from voters who dislike mud-slinging will strike the group sponsoring the ad rather than the candidate supported by the ad. Candidates may reduce their own attacks somewhat because they can rely on these groups to attack opponents. This chapter examines persuasive attacks created and disseminated by two groups during the 2020 election: the Lincoln Project attacking Trump and Republican PACs attacking Biden.

# The Lincoln Project

The Lincoln Project is a PAC founded in 2019 by Republicans to oppose the re-election of President Donald Trump ("The Lincoln Project," 2020). George Conway, one of the founders of this group, is married to Kellyanne Conway, who served as counselor to President Trump (at the end of August 2020, both Conways unexpectedly resigned from their positions; LeBlanc, 2020). The Lincoln Project made and disseminated political spots, most of which criticized President Trump. "Some of the ads were run on TV, on *Fox News*, or in battleground states. Some were simply released online, at a rapid pace" (Weiss, 2020, para 3). The group uses guilt by contrast when it adopts as part of its name the iconic Republican President's name: The *Lincoln* Project. Broadcasting ads on *Fox News* is important if the organization wants to convert some Republicans (and it is possible that the folks at The Lincoln Project also wanted to get under Trump's skin).

These ads reached a very large audience. For example, YouTube views demonstrate that several Lincoln Project advertisements are generating noticeable attention as of July 2, 2020: #TrumpIsNotWell (1.2M views); Tulsa (889K views); Chyna (856K views); Shrinking (1.5M views); Truth (1.3M views); Strong (330K views); Bounty (1.1M views); How a President Leads (848K views); Debt (980K views); Betrayed (831K views); Which Side of History (224K views). Furthermore, the Lincoln Project spot "Betrayed," featuring "former Navy Seal Dan Barkhuff, released Sunday, racked up almost 6 million views on Twitter in the first 24 hours … and another 800,000 on YouTube" (Electoral-vote, 2020). Of course, the YouTube views for the other ads listed above would be augmented with Twitter views. These messages of persuasive attack are significant due to their sizable audience. This chapter examines 20 Lincoln Project attack ads targeted at character and action. These messages criticized the president's character and his policies.

# Attacks on Trump's Character

This section will illustrate a variety of attacks on President Trump's character found in this sample of Lincoln Project PAC ads, including cowardice, incompetence, racism, Putin's puppet, and weakness. Particular attention will be paid to intensifying these criticisms.

## Cowardice

Several of these PAC advertisements vilified President Trump as a coward. For example, "Betrayed" declared that Trump is "a coward" and a "draft dodger" and then suggested that he is "spineless." Similarly, the ad titled "War Zone" explicitly labeled Trump a coward. These accusations are direct and clear. The Lincoln Project also used guilt by contrast in its ad "Mattis": "The coward Trump dodged the draft. Jim Mattis led American troops for 40 years." This message also reported that "a frightened Trump hides from protestors in a deep bunker." Several of these PAC ads charged that President Trump was a coward.

## Incompetence

A second criticism of Trump's character was that he was an incompetent leader. For instance, "Unfit" declared that the president is "unprepared," "untrustworthy," "unaccountable," "uninformed," and "unfit." "Leadership" shows a video of President Trump declaring, "I don't take responsibility at all" for the coronavirus pandemic. This stance is not appropriate for the leader of the United States. The ad "Betrayed" asserted that "Donald Trump is unfit to be our commander-in-chief, and that's worse than useless." In a more extensive and more visual accusation, "Unfit" juxtaposes President Trump's statements with contradictory video clips. Trump is shown saying "We've got it totally under control. It's gonna just be fine," over a background of video and headlines about shutdowns. Trump said, "I think that we're doing a great job," "Take it easy," and "Just relax" as the pandemic grows. Trump's statement that "Anybody that wants a test can get a test" is followed by Vice President Pence saying, "We don't have enough tests." A more global indictment can be found in "Leadership," which criticized the president by stating, "There's mourning in America, and under the leadership of Donald Trump, our country is weaker, sicker, and poorer." This statement alludes to, and contrasts with, a famous ad from President Ronald Reagan seeking reelection by arguing that America was improving: "Morning in America."

The ad "Breaking news: The president does read" reported that White House Press Secretary Kayleigh McEnany said on June 30, "The President does read." This statement responded to a *Washington Post* story that President Trump rarely reads his presidential intelligence briefings (Presidential Daily

Briefs, or PDB); Blake (2020) noted that "The *Post* reported in early 2018 that Trump doesn't read the PDBs." Blake continues his verbal assault by noting:

> It's certainly worth entertaining the possibility that Trump's aversion to detail and to bad news about Russia have conspired to render him hopelessly uninformed about an issue of significant national interest—one involving the lives of U.S. troops, no less. (The intelligence has connected the bounties to actual deaths.)

This attack used humor to make a serious point about President Trump's leadership style.

## Racism

Some spots attacked President Trump for being racist. For instance, "Which Side of History" accused the president of having "racist anger." Another message ("Tulsa") employed video clips to criticize Trump, with video of him saying, "You have to dominate the streets. Please don't be too nice." It also provides video of him declaring that there were "very fine people on both sides" of the 2017 Charlottesville "Unite the Right" white supremacist rally in which a man drove a car into a crowd, killing and injuring bystanders. It also showed a photograph of a Confederate flag with "Trump 2016" printed on it. This attack criticized President Trump for being racist.

These ads intensified this accusation in multiple ways. The ad "Which Side of History" emphasized the extent of the president's racist actions, noting that he tweeted the video of his supporters shouting "White Power" with "millions." Guilt by association was utilized in "Tulsa," where footage of George Wallace declared, "I say segregation now, segregation tomorrow, and segregation forever … I agree that looters ought to be shot … on sight." George Wallace is reviled by many Americans. This spot also displayed guilt by contrast. It used footage from Martin Luther King Jr. saying, "Now is the time to rise from the dark and desolate valley of segregation to the sunlit pass of racial justice." Furthermore, Trump was contrasted with Robert F. Kennedy in "Tulsa": "Too often we honor swagger and bluster and the wielders of force. Too often we excuse those who are willing to build their own lives on the shattered dreams of other human beings." These utterances and strategies combined to attack President Trump as a racist.

## Putin's Puppet

"Fellow Traveler" shows scenes of Trump and Putin (and other visuals) with a narrator speaking Russian. The ad provided "translations" shown on screen (these "translations" were not actual translations, but attacks). One declared that "Donald Trump received the most important endorsement in 2016 from our great leader Vladimir Putin." It went on to explain that Russian "special services worked overtime to elect Comrade Trump." It boasted that "We manipulated your voters, spread our glorious propaganda, and you, American dogs, were set against each other." The translation declared that "now our wise and strong leader, Vladimir Putin, has once again chosen for himself an American ally, Donald Trump. Again!" Finally, this ad averred, "Comrade Trump gladly accepted the help of Mother Russia" and Putin in the 2016 election. Mr. Putin is not considered an ally of America by most people, so this is clearly an example of an attack.

## Weak

Several of these PAC ads portray Donald Trump as weak. For example, "Trump's Wellness" said that Trump is "shaky," "weak," and has "trouble walking," all accompanied by a video of Trump. It made fun of the president for walking up the stairs to Air Force One with toilet paper stuck on his shoe (again illustrated with video). It concluded that America does not need a "weak, unfit, shaky president." The spot "Shrinking" attacked him for poor attendance at his rally in Tulsa on June 20, 2020, which was much smaller than he had promised. This attack implied criticism of his virility. "It was smaller than we expected," "It sure wasn't as big as you promised" "I can't keep your polls up." "Sad. Weak. Low energy" (see also, "Bounty"). President Trump is characterized as the antithesis of a strong leader.

## Other attacks

Finally, several criticisms were not fully developed and will be gathered together in this paragraph. "Distracted" charged that the president did not care about COVID deaths: "When Trump bothered to take it [Covid-19] seriously, it was too late for 10,000 Americans, and who knows how many more. Trump just didn't care. He still doesn't." This attack also employed the strategy of intensifying by extensiveness. The spot "Mattis" featured General

James Mattis declaring that "Donald Trump is the first president in my lifetime who does not try to unite the American people—does not even pretend to try. Instead he tries to divide us." Clearly, uniting America, not dividing it, is what a good president should work toward. The Lincoln Project ad "Truth" called President Trump a liar. Not just an ordinary liar, but "the most deceptive, lying president in history." The use of extent is obvious here, even though it does not use numerical data. Finally, this PAC alleged that Donald Trump was unprincipled. Trump is "corrupt" ("Chyna"). This section shows the variety of attacks leveled by the Lincoln Project against President Donald Trump's character.

## Attacks on Trump's Policy

The Lincoln Project also besmirched several of President Trump's policies. This section discusses four complaints: his failed response to the coronavirus, his failed economy, his failure to object to Russian bounties on American soldiers, and his treatment of peaceful protesters in order to stage a photo opportunity.

### Failed Response to Coronavirus

One of the most important policy criticisms concerned Trump's failure to effectively respond to the pandemic. The ad "Leadership" noted that Trump disbanded the "White House pandemic office." Rather than strengthening our ability to deal with COVID-19, the president weakened our pandemic response infrastructure. "Truth" displayed video of Trump saying,

> When you do testing to that extent, you're gonna find more people, you're gonna find more cases. So I said to my people, slow the testing down, please!" Slow the testing down? Slow down our chance to save tens of thousands of lives [video of patients in hospitals treated by people in hazmat suits]? Slow down our understanding of where Covid is and how it's spreading. Slow down the steps to reopen the economy [Coronavirus pandemic: 26.4 million Americans file for unemployment].

This video makes it clear that the president was upset that testing revealed how widespread the pandemic had become. His "solution" was not to step up the fight against COVID-19, but to slow down testing. This excerpt uses the strategy of extent when it mentions the number of unemployed.

"Mourning in America" uses the extent of damage strategy: "More than 60,000 Americans have died from a deadly virus Donald Trump ignored." As the pandemic death toll mounted, the attacks continued. The advertisement was titled "100,000 dead Americans. One wrong president" ridiculed Donald Trump for saying, "When you have 15 people [infected with coronavirus] and the 15, within a couple of days, is gonna be close to zero." One hundred thousand dead from the Coronavirus is far too many, although unfortunately, the number of dead would continue to rise. This ad campaign combined extent with an emphasis on the effects on the audience: "Millions worry that a loved one won't survive COVID-19" ("Leadership"). We note that as we write this chapter, more than a million Americans have died from the pandemic.

## Failed Economic Policies

A second criticism leveled against Trump by these Republicans concerned the poor economy. "Leadership" blamed Trump for an "economy in shambles; more than 26 million Americans are out of work. The worst economy in decades." These statements illustrate the use of extent to intensify this attack. The ad also derided him because "Trump bailed out Wall Street but not Main Street." This instance of persuasive attack also criticized the current president because "this afternoon millions of Americans will apply for unemployment and, with their savings running out, many are giving up hope" ("Leadership"). President Trump was accused of presiding over an economy that was tanking.

## Failed Response to Russian Bounties on American Soldiers

*The Washington Post* revealed in June 2020 that Russia had offered bounties for killing American soldiers in Afghanistan. The ad "Betrayed" states that President Trump knew about the Russian bounty program but "chose to do nothing about it." Another spot, "Bounty," reported, "Donald Trump knows [Vladimir Putin pays a bounty for the murder of American soldiers] too, and does nothing about it." This attack observed that, "Instead of condemnation, he insists Russia be treated as our equal." The first ad discussed ("Betrayed") also declared that "the lives of our troops depend on" sending Trump back to his golf courses. Finally, the attack declared that "when Trump tells you he stands by the troops, he's right. Just not our troops" (Bounty"). This text hints at another strategy for intensifying an attack without making it explicit: The Commander-in-Chief has an obligation to protect his soldiers.

## Attacked Protesters

The TV spot "War Zone" advanced several attacks pertaining to suppression of protests over George Floyd's death on June 1, 2020, in Lafayette Square, DC, when Donald Trump held up a Bible at St. John's Episcopal Church. The president was accused of having "threatened our governors and our states. He ordered our own soldiers, who fought in Iraq and Afghanistan...to turn against Americans." Trump "ordered an attack on unarmed protesters using gas, rubber bullets, and flash grenades." Furthermore, the spot condemned his use of this situation in Lafayette Square as the backdrop for a photo opportunity. He "used churches and the holy Bible as props. He didn't invoke the Lord to give us wisdom but to boost his polls." His actions that day were held up for ridicule in this persuasive attack. These four accusations illustrate the Lincoln Project's attacks on Trump's policies.

We would also like to note efforts to enhance the credibility of these messages. In "Betrayed," which slams President Trump for doing nothing about the Russian bounties on American soldiers in Afghanistan, Dan Barkhuff tells the audience that "I'm a 2001 United States Naval Academy graduate. I'm an ex-Navy SEAL, currently an emergency room physician." This statement establishes his credentials to comment on military affairs. He also addresses concerns that he might be a liberal: "I'm a pro-life, gun-owning combat veteran." Credibility is an important element in persuasion (see, e.g., Benoit & Benoit, 2008; Benoit & Strathman, 2004), so these statements may reduce the likelihood that his audience will reject his message out of hand.

# Republican PAC Advertisements

TV spots from three more traditional GOP PACS (America First Action, Committee to Defend the President, and Great America) that targeted the Democratic presidential candidate, Joe Biden, were also examined for the use of persuasive attacks. A total of 16 TV spots from these groups comprised the sample used here. These messages, like those from The Lincoln Project, criticized both character and policy. These two topics of attack will be discussed here.

# Attacks on Biden's Character

We identified five criticisms of Vice President Joe Biden's character: untrustworthy, Washington insider, mental capacity, *quid pro quo* Joe (family benefits), and Tara Reade's accusations of sexual assault. Each accusation will be discussed in turn.

## Untrustworthy

"Warned" argued that "we couldn't trust Joe Biden then [when NAFTA was negotiated]. We can't trust him to protect Michigan jobs now." "Joe Biden Can't Be Trusted," not surprisingly, argued that we should not "believe Biden's empty promises." These statements criticize the former vice president for being untrustworthy.

## Washington Insider

The ad "Bad Folks" lamented Biden's "47 years in Washington," while "Poor Michigan" mentioned his "forty years in Washington." The attack in "Toast" ups the tally a bit to "five decades in Washington." The implication here is that Joe Biden is out of touch with voters outside the Beltway. Notice that the excerpts presented below revisit this criticism in the course of attacking Biden's policy.

## Mental Capacity

The spot "Lost His Mind [online version]" asked, "Does Joe Biden have the mental capacity to keep America safe?" It then offered several video claims of Biden mumbling. The spot concluded, "We don't need a president who's already lost his" mind. This theme was addressed in another version of this ad ("Lost His Mind [TV version]"), asking, "Is Joe Biden making any sense?" and "Does Joe Biden have dementia?" These attacks criticize Biden's mental abilities.

## Quid Pro Quo Joe

One spot explained, *quid pro quos*, Biden was said to have obtained for his family.

Weeks after Joe Biden visits China as Vice President, his son secures a private billion dollar deal with a bank in China. After Biden is named America's top diplomat to Ukraine, his son lands another million dollar deal in Ukraine. Then, Biden gets Ukraine's top prosecutor fired before he can investigate ("*Quid Pro Quo* Joe"). The concern raised here is not so much about Biden's foreign policy but about his character because he makes deals to help his family.

## Tara Reade Sexual Assault

An ad from the PAC Great America ("Shattered") reported that "Tara Reade said Joe Biden sexually assaulted her. It used footage from her saying, "He had me up against the wall. And then his hands were on me and underneath my clothes. He went down my skirt but then up inside it. He was kissing me at the same time." The attack noted that "four others have corroborated Reade's story." It discussed the effects on the victim: "Tara Reade's life was shattered." If accepted by viewers, this accusation should damage Biden's reputation.

# Attacks on Biden's Policy

Complaints about Biden's policy tended to center around jobs. Some of these attacks specifically addressed trade with China as well as jobs lost from a ban on fracking.

## Jobs

"No More" argued that "after 47 years in Washington, Joe Biden just doesn't make sense for Pennsylvania jobs." "Toast" declared that "for five decades in Washington, Joe Biden's been wrong on China. Decade after decade, Biden voted for weak, job killing trade deals." This statement alludes to the strategy of intensifying an attack as a repeated offense.

## China

The spot "Competitor" asked, "Is China an ally or a competitor?" Biden answered "neither," which was taken to mean "If you can't understand the threat, you can't stop China." The spot "Poor Michigan" said that "Forty years in Washington, give or take … He spent them supporting trade with China, making friends in China, while over 100,000 Michigan jobs were sent to Chinese factories and Chinese businesses." This jab used the strategy of assessing the extent of damage. It also reported that "the trade deficit... grew by millions." "Competitor" leveled the accusation that "China's been stealing our manufacturing, costing Wisconsin almost 90,000 jobs." This attack also used the idea of effects on the audience. Similarly, "Wrong for So Long" declares that "Joe Biden's trade deals with China cost Wisconsin nearly 89,000 jobs. Then Michigan lost over 160,000 jobs." This statement again explicitly addresses effects on the audience.

## Fracking

"Impact" declared that "Joe Biden wants to eliminate fracking." It included a video clip of the Democrat saying, "We would make sure it's eliminated" (see also "No More"). The effects would be large. "Over 600,000 Pennsylvanians' jobs gone. Billions in wages lost. Thirty thousand retail jobs, history. And 14,000 manufacturing jobs closed down." These statements about effects use the strategy of estimating the extent of the damage. This spot ended with the idea that Biden's goal would have effects on the audience: "He's talking about your job."

# Observations and Conclusions

The Lincoln Project messages displayed greater creativity than the GOP Political Actions Committee spots because they hit Trump harder than we would normally see from members of the same party. What accounts for this disparity? One answer could be that the Lincoln Project PAC had more funds than the other PACs and therefore could hire better consultants, a practice consistent with most large-scale advertising campaigns. It is also possible that President Donald Trump was more susceptible to attacks than Vice President Joe Biden due to his unapologetic and controversial public remarks and handling of various national challenges (e.g., COVID). The president's disapproval rating topped his approval rating on February 3, 2017, and his approval remained underwater for the remainder of the campaign ("How popular or unpopular is Donald Trump?" 2021). Regardless of the extent to which the pandemic was his fault, it happened under his watch, and during most of

2020, the death toll increased steadily as the campaign progressed. In spite of Trump's claims related to election fraud (Cummings et al., 2021), Biden eventually defeated Trump in the popular vote (Biden: 81,268,924 votes, 51.3%; Trump: 74,216,154, 46.9%) and in the Electoral College (Biden: 306, Trump: 232; "2020 United States presidential election," 2021).

Of course, voting is influenced by a plethora of factors, including voters' ideology, news reports, information disseminated by social media, the Internet, and other sources, as well as messages from candidates and other sources, including PACs. Concerns about voting in the midst of a pandemic clearly influenced turnout and perhaps the outcome in 2020. So many elements converge to influence election results that no individual component of the campaign can be singled out as the "cause" of the election outcome. Logic might suggest that traditional GOP ads attacking Biden would be effective in lowering his appeal with voters, which may have occurred to some extent. However, this case suggests that internal party attacks, like those from the Lincoln Project, were slightly more damaging to Trump's cause in an election with razor-thin voting margins in key states. The Lincoln Project ads were noteworthy because they offered attacks on both policy and character. Nguyen and Schneider (2020) argue that these ads were successful because they became a "squatter in Trump's mental space" for several reasons:

> Members each boasting hundreds of thousands of social media followers, rapidly cut ads that respond to current events and a single-minded focus on buying airtime wherever Trump is most likely to be bingeing cable news that day, whether it's the D.C. market or his golf courses across the country. And every time Trump freaks out—or every time the media covers his freakout—the Lincoln Project scores an incalculable amount of earned media, and millions of views online to boot. (para 7)

Analysis of these messages helps us to understand that the role of attacks in a political campaign may not only function to persuade voters but also to antagonize political opponents and their allies by forcing them into reactionary messaging that may conflict with previous depictions of their character or behavior.

# References

America First Action. (2020, April 16). *Bad Folks* [Video]. YouTube. https://www.youtube.com/watch?v=-QoUE4Gk5PM

America First Action. (2020, April 16). *Joe Biden has been wrong for 40 Years* [Video]. YouTube.

America First Action. (2020, May 15). *Coin Flip* [Video]. YouTube. https://www.youtube.com/watch?v=izWcTGMLB1Y

America First Action. (2020, May 15). *Poor Michigan* [Video]. YouTube. https://www.youtube.com/watch?v=Fwx-72A7wLo

America First Action. (2020, May 15). *Toast* [Video]. YouTube. https://www.youtube.com/watch?v=ZNZHrGFjRXQ

America First Action. (2020, June 4). *Competitor* [Video]. YouTube. https://www.youtube.com/watch?v=0-QsXlJQICg

America First Action. (2020, June 4). *One Hundred Sixty Thousand* [Video]. YouTube. https://www.youtube.com/watch?v=LsmQHcOXD3s

America First Action. (2020, June 19). *Impact* [Video]. YouTube. https://www.youtube.com/watch?v=DJdhMdEYG9M

America First Action. (2020, June 19). *Warned* [Video]. YouTube. https://www.youtube.com/watch?v=K393IAQKvM4

America First Action. (2020, June 19). *Wrong for So Long* [Video]. YouTube. https://www.youtube.com/watch?v=Ygb7FkW40YU

America First Action. (2020, October 14). *No More* [Video]. YouTube. https://www.youtube.com/watch?v=SzhqeOmx4CQ

Benoit, W. L. (2014). *A functional analysis of political television advertisements* (2nd ed.). Lexington Books.

Benoit, W. L., & Benoit, P. J. (2008). *Persuasive messages: Balancing influence in communication.* Blackwell.

Benoit, W. L., & Strathman, A. (2004). Source credibility and the elaboration likelihood model. In J. S. Seiter & R. H. Gass (Eds.), *Perspectives on persuasion, social influence, and compliance gaining* (pp. 95–111). Pearson.

Blake, A. (2020, June 30). 2 things that seem to explain Trump's ignorance about Russia's bounties on U.S. troops. *Washington Post.* https://go-gale-com.proxy.library.ohio.edu/ps/retrieve.do?tabID=News&resultListType=RESULT_LIST&searchResultsType=SingleTab&hitCount=1&searchType=AdvancedSearchForm&currentPosition=1&docId=GALE%7CA628142018&docType=Article&sort=Relevance&contentSegment=ZXAY-MOD1&prodId=OVIC&pageNum=1&contentSet=GALE%7CA628142018&searchId=R2&userGroupName=athe17405&inPS=true

Cummings, W., Garrison, J., & Sergent, J. (2021, January 6). By the numbers: President Donald Trump's failed efforts to overturn the election: Trump and allies filed scores of lawsuits, tried to convince state legislatures to take action, organized protests and held hearings.. None of it worked. *USA Today.* https://www.usatoday.com/in-depth/news/politics/elections/2021/01/06/trumps-failed-efforts-overturn-election-numbers/4130307001/

DeYoung, K., Harris, S., Nakasima, E., & Demirjian, K. (2020, June 30). Intelligence reports on Russian bounty operation first reached White House in early 2019. *Washington Post.* https://www.washingtonpost.com/national-security/democrats-assail-administration-officials-for-not-forcing-trump-to-address-russian-operation-targeting-us-troops/2020/06/30/4744f408-badf-11ea-80b9-40ece9a701dc_story.html

Electoral-vote. (2020, July 2). https://electoral-vote.com/

Great America. (2020). *Quid Pro Quo Joe* [Video]. YouTube. https://www.youtube.com/watch?v=oG0t8mIq1Bc

Great America. (2020). *Shattered* [Video]. YouTube. https://www.youtube.com/watch?v=y7dBd1sWQho

How popular/unpopular is Donald Trump? (2021). *FiveThirtyEight*. https://projects.fivethirtyeight.com/trump-approval-ratings/

LeBlanc, P. (2020, August 24). Kellyanne Conway announces she's leaving the White House and George Conway is stepping away from Lincoln Project. *CNN*. https://www.cnn.com/2020/08/23/politics/kellyanne-conway-george-conway-white-house-lincoln-project/index.html

Lincoln Project. (2020, January 9). *The MAGA Church*. [Video]. YouTube. https://www.youtube.com/watch?v=yoglNFN5-Js.

Lincoln Project. (2020, March 17). *Unfit*. [Video]. YouTube. https://www.youtube.com/watch?v=7gJgmkWJ6es

Lincoln Project. (2020, April 9). *Distracted*. [Video]. YouTube. https://www.youtube.com/watch?v=UHjJydZO99A

Lincoln Project. (2020, May 5). Mourning in America. https://www.google.com/search?q=mourning+in+america+lincoln+project+youtube&oq=mourning+in+America+lin&aqs=chrome.2.69i57j0l3.9152j1j7&sourceid=chrome&ie=UTF-8

Lincoln Project. (2020, May 6). *Leadership*. [Video]. YouTube. https://www.youtube.com/watch?v=ZnBRu0ANDIc

Lincoln Project. (2020, May 26). *100,000 dead Americans. One wrong president.* [Video]. YouTube. https://www.youtube.com/watch?v=hitGT3TkP9s

Lincoln Project. (2020, June 3). *War Zone*. [Video]. YouTube. https://lincolnproject.us/news/war-zone/

Lincoln Project. (2020, June 5). *Mattis*. [Video]. YouTube. https://www.youtube.com/watch?v=oYa8mEr3sJA

Lincoln Project. (2020, June 10). *Flag of Treason*. [Video]. YouTube. https://www.youtube.com/watch?v=wFQAYjzLz-c

Lincoln Project. (2020, June 16). *Trump's wellness*. [Video]. YouTube. https://www.youtube.com/watch?v=2JWYSkwpWaY.

Lincoln Project. (2020, June 17). *Tulsa*. [Video]. YouTube. https://www.youtube.com/watch?v=1-g1CVtUX-4

Lincoln Project. (2020, June 17). *Chyna*. [Video]. YouTube.https://www.youtube.com/watch?v=wuAHz4i3_x8

Lincoln Project. (2020, June 22). *Shrinking*. [Video]. YouTube. https://www.youtube.com/watch?v=NOI3ycbaCaE

Lincoln Project (2020, June 23). *Truth*. [Video]. YouTube. https://www.youtube.com/watch?v=vEzfHfLaLG4

Lincoln Project. (2020, July 6). Breaking news: The president does read. https://www.nbcnews.com/politics/donald-trump/how-lincoln-project-anti-trump-republicans-got-his-head-spoiler-n1232669

Morris. R. (1992). Cartoons and the political system: Canada, Quebec, Wales, and England. *Canadian Journal of Communication*, *17*, 253-258.

Nguyen, T. & Schneider, E. (2020, June 27). The Lincoln Project is trolling Trump. But can it sway voters? *Politico*. https://www.politico.com/news/2020/06/27/lincoln-project-trolling-trump-sway-voters-341928

Weiss, J. (2020, July 6). What the Lincoln Project ad makers get about voters (and what Dems don't). *Politico*. https://www.politico.com/news/magazine/2020/07/06/lincoln-project-ads-republicans-democrats-349184

2020 United States presidential election. (2021). *Wikipedia*. https://en.wikipedia.org/wiki/2020_United_States_presidential_election

# · 6 ·

# SOVIET ATTACK IN RESPONSE TO THE 1960 U-2 INCIDENT

On May 1, 1960, a U-2 spy plane piloted by Francis Gary Powers was shot down while on an intelligence-gathering mission over Soviet airspace (Frankel, 1960). Powers was unable to activate a destruction device within the surveillance camera before evacuating the aircraft. The Soviets captured the pilot and collected undamaged portions of the plane ("Excerpts," 1960). The incident was particularly debilitating to US/Soviet relations in the wake of a summit that was scheduled to take place in Paris on May 16th between the United States, the Soviet Union, France, and Britain. At the onset of the summit, Soviet premier Nikita Khrushchev requested to be the first speaker and proceeded to demand an official apology from President Dwight D. Eisenhower for the U-2 overflight. Eisenhower responded that he would end the surveillance flights but refused to apologize or take responsibility for the incident. At that point, the summit ended as Khrushchev refused to continue the dialogue (Beschloss, 1986).

The incident merits scholarly attention for several reasons. Perhaps the most compelling reason for a focus on the U-2 incident is the impact it had on the United States' relations with the Soviet Union at the height of the Cold War. In fact, a chief goal of Eisenhower's political tenure was the preservation of good relations between the two nations. As Beschloss

(1986) explained: "Since January 1953, when he entered office, Eisenhower's chief aspiration had been to build the foundation for an extended improvement in American-Soviet relations. He was uniquely qualified to achieve a détente" (p.6). Eisenhower's military record provided him with an opportunity to negotiate with Khrushchev without appearing politically weak. These conditions paved the way for what might have led to the first Cold War breakthrough: a limited nuclear test ban treaty. The Paris summit would have provided Eisenhower and Khrushchev with an opportunity to finalize the treaty. Khrushchev believed that the flights were not simply immoral but also a deliberate attempt to ruin the summit talks. He labeled them as hostile acts of aggression that were deliberate attempts to sabotage the relaxed international atmosphere. An attack had been made that carried the potential to damage US credibility and also further perpetuate the caution and suspicion with which each nation dealt with the other diplomatically. From an historical perspective, the incident provides interesting lessons regarding the ease with which all progress toward détente could be unraveled.

The incident also posed some interesting rhetorical challenges for those involved. In his attack, Khrushchev deliberately withheld information regarding the status of the plane and the pilot so that the US government would continue to offer its account involving a "weather plane" that strayed off course. In a meeting of the Supreme Soviet in Moscow, Khrushchev stated:

> Comrades, I must tell you a secret. When I was making my report, I deliberately did not say that the pilot was alive and in good health and that we have got parts of the plane. We did so deliberately because had we told everything at once, the Americans would have invented another version. ("Excerpts," 1960, p.24)

Khrushchev knew that the cover story was a lie and allowed the United States to expound upon the lie further to make future denials more difficult. The political forces threatening the leadership of Khrushchev within the Soviet Union as well as the battle for world opinion on the eve of the Paris summit create a unique context likely to put an imprint on any *apologia* offered as a result of the U-2 incident.

# Attack Strategies During the 1960 U-2 Incident

The Soviet Union used a variety of rhetorical strategies in its attack on the United States. All of these arguments support two primary attacks: (1) US espionage is a harmful intrusion into Soviet territory; and (2) the timing of the U-2 flight damaged bilateral relations, resulting in the disruption of the summit meeting. Attack strategies functioned to either increase the overall responsibility of the accused or to increase the overall offensiveness of the act.

# Attack #1: US Espionage is a Harmful Intrusion of Soviet Territory

## Increasing Perceived Responsibility for the Act

The Soviets used three strategies designed to increase responsibility for the act: (1) arguing the accused committed the act before; (2) arguing the accused planned the act; and (3) arguing the accused benefited from the act.

*The accused committed the act before.* The Soviet Union claimed that the United States had violated its airspace repeatedly in an effort to gather intelligence. For example, a telegram from Moscow to the US Department of State on May 10th, published the next day in all three major American newspapers, stated: "Hostile acts of American aviation, which have taken place numerous times in relation to Soviet Union, are not simply result of activity of military commands of USA in various areas, but are expressions of a calculated US policy" ("Incoming Telegram," 1960). The Soviets emphasized the culpability of the United States by arguing that surveillance was occurring with great frequency and that oversight of US activities was not limited to the military but a "calculated policy" of the United States. Political candidate Sharmazanashvili reiterated the argument by quantifying the amount of US spying prior to the May 1st incident:

> Such violations of the air space of other states are not isolated instances in U.S. practice. For example, between 1953 and 1956 planes of the United States of America intruded 113 times in the air space of the U.S.S.R. and 211 times in the air space of the European people's democracies. In subsequent years these repeated attempts at intrusion in the air space of the U.S.S.R. did not cease, a fact particularly evident through the violation of the air space of the U.S.S.R by an American plane on April 9, 1960 as well. ("News of the Week," 1960, p.32)

Sharmazanashvili lamented the excessive number of intrusions into Soviet airspace by specifying how often these flights occurred.

Additionally, the Soviets did not rely exclusively on Russian accounts of US spying to make the argument. They claimed that Powers had testified about the frequency of the spying. Khrushchev argued in a speech to the Supreme Soviet on May 7th: "He himself [Powers] said, he had flown along the Soviet border many times in order to study the Soviet Union's radar systems" ("Khrushchev's Closing," 1960, p.5). Khrushchev utilized the testimony of Powers to support his argument that "many" flights had taken place over the USSR. Khrushchev also highlighted US espionage in other countries, particularly Austria:

> Suffice it to recall the flight of American military planes over the territory of Austria when aggression was being prepared against Iraq, where a revolution had just taken place. The Austrian government protested against perfidious violation of Austria's sovereignty by American military planes. ("Khrushchev's Closing," 1960, p.5)

Khrushchev's examples of US surveillance in neighboring countries elevated the level of responsibility by the United States because they showed that the spying activity was neither limited to a single incident (the U-2 incident) nor limited to a single country (the Soviet Union).

*The accused planned the act.* The Soviets argued that the United States planned the reconnaissance missions by providing explanations of the possible motivations behind the spying. The first evidence used to illustrate the intentionality of US activity was the distance of the plane into Soviet territory before it was finally shot down. The Soviets argued that a plane veering more than 2,000 km off course could only do so deliberately. For example, a telegram from Moscow to the United States on May 10th argued:

> On May 1 of this year at 5 hour 36 minutes, Moscow time, a military aircraft violated the boundary of the Union of Soviet Socialist Republics and intruded across the borders of the Soviet Union for a distance of more than 2,000 kilometers. When the intentions of the violating aircraft became apparent, it was shot down by Soviet rocket troops in the area of Sverdlovsk. ("Incoming Telegram," 1960)

The note suggested that the final location of the crashed aircraft, deep in sovereign territory, was evidence of US intentions to spy on the Soviet Union.

The Soviets also used Powers' testimony once again to support premeditation by the United States. The May 10th telegram from Moscow argued:

> The pilot has indicated that he did everything in full accordance with assignment given him. On the flight map taken from him there was clearly and accurately marked the entire route he was assigned after takeoff from the city of Adana (Turkey), Peshawar (Pakistan) – the Ural Sea – Sverdlovsk – Archangel – Murmansk, followed by a landing at the Norwegian airfield at Bude. ("Incoming Telegram," 1960)

The telegram established that Powers was given a very specific assignment, which involved aerial surveillance over designated portions of the Soviet Union. The existence of physical evidence (a flight map) strengthened the attack.

The telegram also referred to technology found on the plane as well as photographs of Russian terrain as evidence of US intentions:

> This aircraft was specifically equipped for reconnaissance and diversionary flight over the territory of the Soviet Union. It had on board apparatus for aerial photography, for detecting soviet radar network and other special radio-technical equipment which form part of the U.S.S.R. anti-aircraft defenses. At the disposal of Soviet expert commission which carried out the investigation, there is indisputable proof of the espionage-reconnaissance mission of the American aircraft: Films of Soviet defense and industrial establishments, a tape recording of signals of Soviet radar stations and other data. ("Incoming Telegram," 1960)

The statement very clearly outlined the specific technologies present on the U-2, such as film and radio equipment, which established the planned nature of the flight. The evidence also suggested that the technology was used to gather sensitive information about Soviet defense capabilities. This argument increased responsibility for the act because it demonstrated that the United States would not have possessed such high-tech equipment if its intentions were not premeditated.

Besides arguing that the United States planned the U-2 flight, the Soviet government also claimed that the United States planned to continue such flights. Soviet Foreign Minister Andrei Gromyko argued on May 28th: "President Eisenhower has made it clear that the United States will continue acts of espionage and sabotage against the Soviet Union" ("World on Brink," 1960, p.1A). Gromyko elevated the offensiveness of US actions by making the claim that espionage against the Soviet Union will persist into the future. If the May 1st incident alone was enough to assign blame, then a claim of possible future violations would likely magnify the perceived responsibility for the act even further.

*The accused knew the consequences.* Soviet leaders also attacked the United States by arguing that the US government was aware of the consequences of violating the sovereign territory of the Soviet Union. A telegram from Moscow on May 10th indicated: "The government of the United States of America, instead of taking measures to stop such actions by American aviation, the danger of which has more than once been pointed out by the Soviet government, officially announces such action as its national policy" ("Incoming Telegram," 1960). By arguing that the US government had been informed of the dangers of its behavior, the utterance increased the level of responsibility because it is often perceived as much worse to knowingly commit a harmful act than to do so unknowingly.

*Inconsistency of the offender.* The Soviets argued that the US government was behaving inconsistently in two ways. First, the Soviets argued that the US government was hypocritical because it would never allow aerial surveillance over the United States, but justified its own reconnaissance over the USSR. In his May 7th speech to the Supreme Soviet, Khrushchev said, "I want once again to ask those who are offended what their reaction would be if a plane of ours intruded into the U.S.A. and flew over their territory a distance of about 2000 kilometers." ("Khrushchev Closing," 1960, p.26). In another statement, he argued: "Just imagine what would have been the reaction if, on the eve of my visit to America, we had sent a plane over the United States" (Folliard, 1960, p.A8). These arguments elevated the offensiveness of US actions by showing that the United States would likely hold other countries to a different standard than itself.

Second, Soviet officials argued that US actions were inconsistent with the Christian beliefs espoused by many of its citizens. For example, in his May 7th speech to the Supreme Soviet, Khrushchev argued:

> They consider themselves Christians and believers. They—believers—accuse us of atheism. Excellent indeed is the morality of such people. If such people really believed in God, they would at least be afraid of hell, where they will inevitably end up, because according to the Christian teaching they are destined to boil in pitch in hell eternally for their foul deeds against peace and mankind. No, it is not Christian ethics these people preach. They preach the ethics of the bourgeois world, for which nothing is sacred. ("Khrushchev's Closing," 1960, p.7)

Here, Khrushchev is adamant that the actions of the US government are inconsistent with the values promoted within Christian doctrine. The statement increased the offensiveness of the U-2 incident because it showed that it is objectionable for a government to behave in ways that are inconsistent with the values it promotes.

## Increasing Offensiveness of the Act

One strategy used by the Soviet Union to elevate the offensiveness of the U-2 flight was to show the extent of the damage caused by the incident. Soviet leaders first argued that the event was a precursor to a full-scale war between the two nations:

> Thus the threat of incursion by American aircraft into the air space of other states has not been removed and the threat remains that such acts might lead to serious military clashes and to the unleashing of a nuclear missile war with grave consequences for all humanity. ("Explanatory Note," 1960, p.34)

Khrushchev stressed that nuclear war might be the inevitable result of aerial intrusions into the sovereign territory of another nation. These military clashes could result from retaliation for the flight itself or from retaliation following the accidental release of nuclear missiles during an intelligence-gathering mission. This increased the overall offensiveness of US actions by illustrating the extent of damage that could result from surveillance activities.

Besides simply implying that war might result, the Soviet leaders frequently provided more overt threats to retaliate against the United States for its intrusion into the sovereign territory of the USSR. In his May 10th telegram to the United States, Khrushchev threatened retaliation: "The government of the Soviet Union ... warns that, if similar provocations are repeated, it will be obliged to take retaliatory measures" ("Incoming Telegram," 1960). Although Khrushchev did not specify the nature of the retaliation, he did emphasize that there would be serious "consequences" to future American aggression against the Soviet Union. His threats elevated the level of offensiveness because they established that the act was harmful enough to justify countermeasures as significant as military retaliation.

# Attack #2: The United States Damaged Relations and Disrupted the Summit

The Soviets also argued that the U-2 incident had damaged US–Soviet relations, resulting in the disruption of the Paris summit. They increased US responsibility for the damage by arguing that the accused planned the act.

## Increasing Responsibility for the Act

*Planned the act.* One way in which the Soviets increased US responsibility for the U-2 incident was to provide motivations behind the act. They argued that the United States was attempting to return the state of relations between the two countries to the worst times of the Cold War by exacerbating the atmosphere of mistrust. For example, Khrushchev made the following statement at the airport in Moscow, just before traveling to the Paris summit:

> Although all peoples undoubtedly desire the strengthening of peace and a relaxation of international tension, it is generally known that influential circles that are trying to revive the "cold war" and impede an improvement of the international situation have noticeably intensified their activities in certain countries, especially in the recent period. ("Reporting of the Summit," 1960)

Khrushchev's implication was that the motivation behind recent surveillance flights was to renew international tensions. He established US responsibility for the incident by identifying its motives. This statement did not speculate as to the reasons behind US efforts to strain relations with the Soviet Union, but the use of the term "trying" clearly implied intent behind US actions.

Soviet leaders also argued that the flight of the U-2 was planned to disrupt the summit meeting to be held just 15 days after the plane was shot down. In a transcript published on May 6th of a meeting of the Supreme Soviet, Deputy Tashenev argued: "At such a crucial point, when all mankind is placing large hopes in the forthcoming conference of the leaders of the four great powers, the actions of the American government [aerial surveillance] are in effect aimed at torpedoing that conference" ("Supreme Soviet Discussion," 1960, p.10). Tashenev's use of the term "aimed" clearly implied a US intention to destroy the summit meeting. His use of the metaphor involving a "torpedoing" of the conference added hostility to US efforts to ruin the conference and was consistent with earlier Soviet complaints of American militarist circles seeking to return the state of relations to a more warlike atmosphere. Again, this statement furthered the Soviet argument that the U-2 flight was designed for the purpose of disrupting the summit by identifying a possible motivation behind the act.

## Increasing Offensiveness of the Act

In addition to the strategies designed to increase US responsibility for the damage to bilateral relations prior to the summit, the Soviets also increased the level of offensiveness of the harm by arguing that the United States was inconsistent in its approach to international relations with the Soviet Union.

*Inconsistency of the offender.* First, they argued that the United States claimed it wanted to improve relations with the Soviet Union but deliberately put those relations at risk by engaging in surveillance activities. In his May 10th telegram to the US State Department, Khrushchev argued:

> One must ask, how is it possible to reconcile this with declarations on the part of leading figures of the U.S.A., that the government of the U.S.A., like the Soviet government, also strives for improvement of relations between the U.S.S.R. and the U.S.A., for the relaxation of international tension, and the strengthening of trust between states. The military intelligence activities of one nation by means of intrusion of its aircraft into the area of another country can hardly be called a method for improving relations and strengthening trust. ("Incoming Telegram," 1960)

Khrushchev argued that the behavior of the US government did not match the rhetoric it delivered on easing international tensions between the two nation-states. This increased the offensiveness of the U-2 incident because it showed that the United States was willing to speak out publicly in support of improved relations and then blatantly violate its assurances to the Soviet Union.

# Observations and Conclusions

The Soviet Union's persuasive attack against the United States during the 1960 U-2 incident was internally consistent and plausible. The accusation that the surveillance was a harmful intrusion into Soviet territory was generally well conceived. When the Soviets claimed that the US government had perpetrated numerous intrusions into Soviet airspace, this magnified the level of culpability because it preempted a potential US argument that these flights only occurred on rare occasions. Adding to the effectiveness of the argument was the Soviets' use of evidence to support it. They relied on the testimony of Powers, who clearly stated that he had flown many of these missions. They also provided examples of specific dates on which Soviet territory was violated, as well as examples of other European countries, besides the USSR, that had been targets of espionage.

The Soviet argument that the U-2 flight itself was planned for the purpose of gathering intelligence was probably effective for all audiences, in part, for the same reasons as the previous argument. They utilized the testimony of Powers, who provided Soviet leaders with a map of his flight plan. Additionally, specialized equipment on the plane and surveillance photographs taken of Soviet defense systems provided compelling evidence of the premeditated nature of US activities. Any time evidence can be mustered to support an attack, it is inherently more persuasive. Even Eisenhower conceded years later that the evidence at the time was too compelling to dispute:

> In the diplomatic field it was routine practice to deny responsibility for an embarrassing occurrence when there is even a one percent chance of being believed, but when the world can entertain not the slightest doubt of the facts, there is no point in trying to evade the issue. (Rosenberg, 2005, p.233)

This statement illustrates how well-supported the Soviet argument was regarding the purpose of the U-2 flight. Eisenhower admitted that there really was no way of getting around the evidence. This may have been the reason that the United States was eventually forced to abandon its initial denials in favor of a more conciliatory defensive strategy.

In elevating the U-2 incident's overall level of offensiveness, Soviet leaders indicated that the act was significant enough to be an impetus to war. As a whole, Khrushchev's threats may have appeared excessive to the United States as well as its Western allies, as he threatened to destroy every foreign base that allowed US aircraft to launch and to send nuclear bombs to the United States "in the first minutes" of a war. The tone of the attack with regard to the nuclear threats pointed to a lack of composure and objectivity from Khrushchev.

The Soviet argument suggesting inconsistency on the part of the US government for claiming it wanted good bilateral relations may have been effective in elevating the offensiveness of the U-2 flight because it made the American people appear hypocritical. The argument was consistent with Soviet arguments that the US government planned the act to sabotage the summit and bilateral relations. A logical conclusion was that the US leaders were not completely truthful about wanting good relations and deliberately destroyed them, rather than the destruction of relations as a side effect of an unfortunate surveillance incident. Purposefully lying about subversive intentions is certainly worse than accidentally hurting relationships.

Elements of the Soviet Union's second accusation regarding US intentions to destroy bilateral relations may have been persuasive to Soviet audiences but were clearly ineffectual next to US pre-emptive arguments regarding its "weather plane." If US officials really intended to get caught disrupting relations and the summit, they would never have denied that the purpose of the U-2 flight was to breach Soviet territory. It is somewhat surprising that Khrushchev made this argument after the initial US denial, which may indicate that he wanted to accuse the United States of disrupting relations on the eve of the conference. The Soviet rhetoric suggesting that US activities were "aimed" at disrupting the summit showed that Khrushchev did not see the damage to relations as an unforeseen consequence of surveillance, but as an intended result.

Khrushchev attempted to constrain the *apologia* that was to follow his attack by omitting details that would have allowed the US government an opportunity to develop a more cogent response. In this way, Khrushchev concerned himself not simply with strategies that would increase perceptions of responsibility and offensiveness for the harmful act but would ensure a weakened response. This effort to control the rhetorical response was an illuminating component of the 1960 U-2 incident and may be present in other case studies.

This case also shows the importance of utilizing both responsibility and negative perceptions together to bolster the attack. Here, the Soviets emphasized the extent of the damage by arguing US actions were putting the two countries on a collision course for war. Moreover, they also increased negative perceptions by arguing that the United States was making inconsistent statements about the purpose of the flight. This particular case transcends the theory of attack because it is a reminder that international discourses naturally divide communication based on issues of cultural translation and a strong sense of nationalism. Thus, strategies that are entirely plausible can be rendered ineffective simply because of an audience's predisposition to judge the strategies independent of the message content.

# References

Beschloss, M. R. (1986). *Mayday the U-2 affair: The untold story of the greatest US-USSR spy scandal.* Harper & Row.

Excerpts from Premier Khrushchev's remarks on U.S. jet downed in Soviet. (1960, May 8). *The New York Times,* p.24.

Explanatory note to the U.N. Security Council. (1960, May 18). *Current Digest of the Soviet Press, 12* (20), p.34.

Folliard, E. T. (1960, May 12). Khrushchev doubts Ike welcome in Soviet Union now. *Washington Post,* p.A8.

Frankel, M. (1960, May 6). Rocket downed jet, Soviet says. *The New York Times,* p.1.

Incoming telegram from Moscow. (1960, May 10). U.S. Department of State. http://www.state.gov

Khrushchev's closing speech to Supreme Soviet on U-2. (1960, May 7). *Current Digest of the Soviet Press, 12* (19), p.5.

News of the week: The U-2 incident. (1960, May 20). *Current Digest of the Soviet Press, 12* (22), p.32.

Reporting of the summit conference events in Paris. (1960, May 14). *Current Digest of the Soviet Press, 12* (20), p.3.

Rosenberg, V. (2005). *Soviet–American Relations, 1953–1960.* McFarland and Company.

Supreme Soviet discussion of Khrushchev's report. (1960, May 6). *CurrentDigest of the Soviet Press, 12* (19), p.10.

World on brink of war, Gromyko warns U.N. (1960, May 27). *Los Angeles Times,* p.1A.

# PERSUASIVE ATTACK IN POLITICAL CARTOONS

Political cartoons are a distinctive and significant element of public discourse generally, as well as in specific contexts, such as politics. Scholars often highlight the ability of political cartoons to communicate visually. Bush (2013) considered the history of political cartoons, explaining that these messages "combine metaphors, symbols, and other pictorial representations with text" (p.87). Morrison (1969), as well as Feng and O'Halloran (2013), emphasized the significance of the visual aspects of political cartoons. Cahn (1984) argued that cartoonists rely on visual properties that can be understood by everyone. Cartoons allow people to take in at a glance the meaning of an event or person (Streicher, 1965). The fact that political cartoons offer humorous takes on controversial topics may encourage people to let their guard down, making them more susceptible to the persuasion that inhabits these messages.

Some articles discuss the basic nature of political cartoons. Medhurst and DeSousa (1981) observed four recurrent themes: political commonplaces, literary and cultural allusions, personal character traits, and situational themes. Bostdorff (1987) utilized Burkean rhetorical theory to understand the form and function of political cartoons. Edwards (1997) studied political cartoons that addressed the 1988 presidential campaign, using three different ways to appreciate these messages: image, metaphor, and narrative. Bormann et al.

(1978) employed rhetorical vision/fantasy theme analysis to identify fantasy themes in political cartoons about the 1976 presidential campaign.

Thibodeau (1989) observed that cartoons provide negative depictions of their subjects. Similarly, Cahn (1984) argued that almost all political cartoons were negative because they represented the biased point of view of the cartoonist. Morris (1992) analyzed political cartoons originating in Canada and the United Kingdom, reporting that these messages often attack the democratic and public decision-making process. Becker's (1996) investigation of Soviet cartoons found that party and governmental policy influenced the nature of cartoons. Carl (1970) noted that cartoon readers may not necessarily interpret cartoons as they were intended by the cartoonist, suggesting that no two people interpret a cartoon in precisely the same way, indicating that cartoons are polysemic.

Benoit et al. (2001) conducted a rhetorical vision/fantasy theme analysis of political cartoons lampooning Ken Starr's investigation of Bill Clinton and Monica Lewinsky. The cartoonists' vision lamented the fact that America's public figures (Clinton, Starr, Congress, and news anchors) were engaged in a tawdry drama. These messages were highly visual, metaphorical, and typically critical, allowing for multiple interpretations by audience members.

Benoit and Stein (2009) studied political cartoons that attacked the Catholic Church for sex abuse scandals. They noted three important attacks on the Catholic Church: Catholic priests sexually abused children, the Catholic Church covered up the scandal, and the Church's response to sexual abuse was ineffectual. Kelley-Romano and Westgate (2007) examined political cartoons about President Bush and Hurricane Katrina, which attacked the president for his indecisiveness in handling the crisis; the cartoons suggested that he lacked integrity and intelligence. Wiid et al. (2011) investigated political cartoons targeting three American politicians (Eliot Spitzer, Bill Clinton, and John Edwards). They identify three factors that can influence how politicians are affected by a scandal: the nature of the scandal, the location of the scandal, and the identity of the protagonists in the story.

Benoit and Glantz (2017) analyzed political cartoons that attacked Donald Trump during the 2016 presidential primary campaign. They reported that, collectively, these messages attacked Trump's policy proposals (such as building a wall between the United States and Mexico) and criticized him by using both guilt by association and guilt by contrast. These cartoons repeatedly targeted the Republican candidate's character, portraying him as "insulting, narcissistic, racist, misogynist, empty-headed, not credible, clownish, a windbag, juvenile, vulgar, mentally deficient, and dangerous" (pp. 100–101). These messages provided a barrage of attacks on the eventual GOP nominee.

This chapter will examine political cartoons attacking the two most recent American presidents, Donald Trump (45th President) and Joe Biden (46th President), a Republican and a Democrat, respectively. This analysis used a convenience sample of cartoons obtained via Internet searches; thus, our conclusions cannot be generalized to all Trump and Biden cartoons, let alone all political cartoons. Nevertheless, this analysis will illuminate the use of persuasive attacks in these kinds of messages. We examine cartoons that criticize the earlier president first and then look at cartoons that attack the current president.

## Political Cartoons Attacking President Donald Trump

Political cartoons criticized Donald Trump on three key topics: lies, coronavirus failures, and Russian bounties on American troops in Afghanistan.

## Trump's Lies

Cathey (2021) concluded that Trump's presidency was "riddled" with lies; he told over 30,500 false or misleading claims during his presidency. Cartoonists jumped on this accusation with both feet. Trump was portrayed as flushing the truth down the toilet (Luckovich, 2019). MacGregor (2018) drew several people with elongated noses, declaring that "When it comes to the truth, size matters." In order from longest to shortest nose, we see Trump, Putin, Sessions, Giuliani, Nixon, and Pinocchio. Catalino (2020) portrayed the president saying, "Just because I lied 16,000 times, I'm not lying about Bolton now." The caption declared: "16001," labeling this as another falsehood in a long line of lies. Esquivel (2018) draws Trump with an exceptionally long nose; Pinocchio, shown with a somewhat smaller nose, gazes at Trump adoringly. Obviously, the wooden boy envies Trump's accomplishments as a liar. The Pinocchio character, taken from a 1940 Disney film, was a wooden puppet who yearned to be human, but each time he lied, his nose increased in length. Similarly, the cartoon depicts President Trump with the same condition, clearly indicating that Trump is nothing more than a puppet.

Figure 7.1. Trump and Pinocchio (2018). Reproduced with permission from Visual Image Communications.

The allusions to Pinocchio enact the strategy of the extent of the behavior as Trump's nose is drawn at extreme lengths (Figure 7.1).

## Coronavirus Failures

Ortiz (2021) reported that President Trump was responsible for "more than 400,000 deaths from one event on his watch." A popular topic in memes about Trump was his alleged failures in dealing with COVID-19. Zyglist (2020) depicted Trump as throwing a ball (labeled COVID-19) toward a hoop. He missed the basket but declared that he "nailed it." Another cartoon depicts a chart of coronavirus deaths (going up sharply); Trump (with tiny hands a swipe about his manhood) misinterprets the graph as concerning his ratings (Whamond, 2020a). Woodward revealed that Trump downplayed the virus; Trump explained that he did not want to cause panic ("Trump tells Woodward," 2020). A cartoon by Sutton (2020) showed Trump speaking to the graves of COVID victims, asking, "Aren't you glad I kept you from panicking? I don't get enough credit for that; I really don't." The many coronavirus graves enact the strategy of increasing offensiveness using the extent of damage. Another cartoon shows the coronavirus as a tidal wave (Cagle,

2020), implementing extent again. Another cartoon by Whamond (2020b) characterizes a visit by Trump to a COVID patient (Figure 7.2).

This cartoon draws together several ideas. The chart at the foot of the bed shows coronavirus patients declining over time. Trump is shown with golf clubs, suggesting that he is not spending his full time on the pandemic. He throws a roll of toilet paper (which was in short supply during the national lockdown). This alludes to the time he threw rolls of paper towels during a visit to Puerto Rico after Hurricane Maria. Thus, political cartoons ridiculed Trump in his response to the COVID-19 pandemic.

## Russian Bounties on American Soldiers

Reports in 2020 indicated that Russia put bounties on American troops in Afghanistan (Cummings, 2020). Later reports questioned these allegations, but several cartoons poked fun at the president on this topic when these accusations emerged. A cartoon from Weyant (2020) depicted Trump talking to an American soldier in Afghanistan who had a target on his back. Trump was shown saying, "Relax! Putin told me in Russian it means fake news." This

Figure 7.2. Trump and COVID Patient (2020). Reproduced with permission from Visual Image Communications.

message reminded readers of this allegation and suggested that Trump accepted Putin's denial. Crowe (2020) published a cartoon that showed Putin with two puppets on his knees, a Taliban leader (probably Abdul Ghani Baradar), and Trump. Putin's arm reaches inside Trump's back, implying that Trump is Putin's ventriloquist dummy. In response to a question about whether Russia offered the Taliban a bounty to kill American soldiers, and consistent with the idea that Trump was Putin's puppet, the President said, "Nyet – I mean hoax." The fact that Trump's initial answer was "no" in Russian further attacks the president. A third example of this criticism of the president occurred in a cartoon by Horsey (2020).

This message shows an outraged American soldier reading a poster announcing that Russia would pay bounties to the Taliban for killing American soldiers (Figure 7.3). When asked if he had read it, Trump responded, "Nyet." Again, showing Trump denying the allegation in Russian reinforces the attack.

Figure 7.3. Bounties on US Soldiers (2020). Reproduced with permission from Visual Image Communications.

# Political Cartoons Attacking President Joe Biden

Joe Biden has also been attacked in many political cartoons. This chapter examines attacks in these messages on three topics: Biden's age, his creepy behavior, and gaffes (e.g., plagiarism).

## Biden is Old

Neither Joe Biden nor Donald Trump were spring chickens. As Donovan-Smith observed in November 2020, "Trump, 74, already set the record as the oldest president at inauguration in 2017. Biden … will turn 78 before Inauguration Day." Biden was attacked for his age in memes. During the Democratic presidential primary, Hands (2020a) drew both Bernie Sanders and Joe Biden as old men under the caption "Grumpiest Old Men." Once the general election commenced, Walters (2020) drew a movie marquee with the legend: "Grumpy Old Men: Trump Biden." A cartoon by Knight (2020) depicted the "frontrunner" Biden in a motorized wheelchair with Vice President Kamala Harris riding on the back as his nurse. The pair were ahead of Trump in a limousine.

Biden's age is shown in several ways. He looks old, is dressed in pajamas and a robe, and is driving a wheelchair, with a nurse in attendance (Figure 7.4).

## Biden is Creepy

Some thought that Joe Biden was a little "touchy" around women. For example, a pro-Trump political action committee deployed a TV spot ("Creepy Joe Biden") attacking Joe Biden amid "accusations that he inappropriately touched women" (Tillett, 2019). Memes followed the lead of this advertisement. Stiglich (2019) drew a cartoon of Biden sniffing a woman's hair. He said, "I'm thinking about running," and she said, "That makes two of us." Clearly, the woman was uncomfortable with Biden's behavior: He was talking about running for president, and she was thinking about running away from him. A similar cartoon showed Biden rubbing Amy Klobuchar's shoulders while thanking her for dropping out of the primary race and endorsing him (Hands, 2020b). She does not look pleased with his massage (Figure 7.5).

Figure 7.4. Biden in Motorized Wheelchair (2020). Reproduced with permission from Visual Image Communications

Fitzsimmons (2019) published a cartoon of two women holding signs. One sign said #MeToo. The second woman's sign read "#MeEwww" and said, "I'm just totally creeped out by Biden." This message slams Biden as creepy and implies that he has committed sexual misconduct. These and other political cartoons depicted Biden's social behaviors as disturbing.

## Biden's Gaffes

Biden has committed a number of gaffes over the years. For example, he once said, "You cannot go into a 7-Eleven or a Dunkin' Donuts unless you have a slight Indian accent," which sounds racist, and he explained that FDR talked about the 1929 stock market crash on television, which sounds ignorant (Frantzich, 2020). McKee (2019) drew a press conference for Biden, who stood behind a podium. Microphones were set up in two places: in front of his mouth and behind him (implying that Biden talked out of his behind). A cartoon by Jones (2012) showed Biden with an extremely long tongue, which looped around his neck, suggesting he choked on his words. Cagle (2019) depicted Biden with a donkey (representing the Democratic Party) installing a personal and permanent teleprompter. This attack dates back to 1987, when

Figure 7.5. Creepy Biden (2019). Reproduced with permission from Visual Image Communications.

Joe Biden abandoned his campaign for the 1988 Democratic nomination. He plagiarized a speech (and gestures) from a British politician, Neil Kinnock (Satija, 2019). Not surprisingly, this attack surfaced in memes during Biden's run for the Oval Office in 2020 (Figure 7.6).

The implication here is that it is dangerous to the Democratic Party for Biden to speak on his own. So, political cartoons criticized Biden for his gaffes.

## Observations and Conclusions

Political cartoons are an important means of making a persuasive attack. They do so with humor, which may make them more palatable than other kinds of attacks with some members of the audience. Of course, in today's highly polarized American political scene, some partisans are simply not persuadable. The persuasive attacks in these messages illustrate intensifying criticism using the strategy of assessing the extent of the harm. These messages are quite similar to memes: Political cartoons are visual with a short text and rely on cultural

Figure 7.6. Biden's gaffe problem solved (2019). Reproduced with permission from Visual Image Communications.

stereotypes. For example, most people are familiar with the story of Pinocchio, so an unnaturally elongated nose signals a liar. These cultural icons employed in both political cartoons and memes allow the authors to evoke a disproportionate amount of meaning in recipients. Like memes, political cartoons can appear on the Internet and spread via social media.

Throughout political history, there has always been a risk of audience backlash for attacking too strongly (Verhulsdonk et al., 2022). Therefore, attacks containing humor might generate less animosity from audiences because the attacker could claim to be speaking in gesture. Thus, the cartoons mentioned here may fuel the attacks against Trump disproportionately since he has a hard time dealing with criticism. For example, Newt Gingrich said, "There is a side of Little Trump's personality, particularly to anything which attacks his own sense of integrity or his own sense of respectability, and he reacts very intensely, almost uncontrollably, to those kinds of situations" (McCaskill, 2016, para. 3). Trump is likely to respond to attacks of all kinds, even superficial ones, as equally insulting.

So, these attacks may be more damaging because reacting too harshly to a friendly jab may make you look irrational, incapable of laughing at yourself, or truly have something to hide. A natural extension of this process points to the idea that if you are incapable of any type of surface criticism, you probably lack interpersonal skills that might be needed for leadership or political diplomacy. Biden is not immune to such attacks either, particularly those that deal with the inevitable impact of age. The natural process of change in mobility, weakened memory, or slowed response time can suggest that a person is unfit for such an important office.

Humorous attacks have the potential to make the same arguments as serious ones because they insulate the perpetrator from responsibility for offering unfair or inaccurate attacks. Humorous attacks likely require less evidentiary support compared to other attacks, and there is some evidence to suggest they are equally effective (Verhulsdonk et al., 2022). Thus, the impact of humor has the potential to go beyond a cheap old-age joke without embracing the consequences that standard news reporting requires.

# References

Allen, F., & Schouten, F. (2016, October 8). Trump apologizes for video bragging about groping women. *USA Today*. http://www.usatoday.com/story/news/politics/onpolitics/ 2016/10/07/ trump-washington-post-women-billy-bush-video/91743992/

Associated Press. (2021, April 15). White House: Intel on Russian "bounties" on US troops shaky. https://apnews.com/article/joe-biden-donald-trump-afghanistan-russia-vladimir-putin-928ebdf775268b10e121d3160af2da42

Becker, J. A. (1996). A disappearing enemy: The image of the United States in Soviet political cartoons. *Journalism and Mass Communication Quarterly, 73*, 609–619.

Benoit, W. L., & Glantz, M. (2017). *Persuasive attack on Donald Trump in the 2016 Republican primaries*. Lexington Books.

Benoit, W. L., & Stein, K. A. (2009). *Kategoria* of cartoons on the Catholic Church sexual abuse scandal. In J. R. Blaney & J. P. Zompetti (Eds.), *The rhetoric of Pope John Paul II* (pp. 23–35). Rowman & Littlefield.

Benoit, W. L., Klyukovski, A. A., McHale, J. P., & Airne, D. (2001). A fantasy theme analysis of political cartoons on the Clinton-Lewinsky-Starr affair. *Critical Studies in Media Communication, 18*, 377–394.

Bormann, E. G., Koester, J., & Bennet, J. (1978). Political cartoons and salient rhetorical fantasies: An empirical analysis of the '76 presidential campaign. *Communication Monographs, 45*, 317–329.

Bostdorff, D. M. (1987). Making light of James Watt: A Burkean approach to the form and attitude of political cartoons. *Quarterly Journal of Speech, 73*, 43–59.

Bush, L. (2013). More than words: Rhetorical constructs in American political cartoons. *Studies in American Humor, 3*, 63–91.

Cagle, D. (2019, August 16). 7 scorching cartoons about Joe Biden's gaffe spectacular. *The Week*. https://theweek.com/articles/859289/7-scorching-cartoons-about-joe-bidens-gaffe-spectacular

Cagle, D. (2020, March 28). Daryl Cagle: The great wave of COVID-19 is coming. *Noozhawk*. https://www.noozhawk.com/daryl_cagle_the_great_wave_of_covid_19_is_coming_20200328/

Cahn, D. (1984). The political cartoon as communication. *Media Development, 4,* 39–42.

Carl, L. M. (1968). Editorial cartoons fail to reach many readers. *Journalism Quarterly, 45,* 533–535.

Carl, L. M. (1970). Political cartoons: Ink blots of the editorial page. *Journal of Popular Culture, 4,* 39–45.

Catalino, K. (2020). 16,001. *The Mercury News*. https://www.mercurynews.com/2020/01/28/cartoons-trump-legal-team-presents-impeachment-case-defense/

Cathey, L. (2021, January 20). Legacy of lies – how Trump weaponized mistruths during his presidency. *ABC News*. https://abcnews.go.com/Politics/legacy-lies-trump-weaponized-mistruths-presidency/story?id=75335019

Crowe, J. D. (2020, July 3). The Taliban Putin and Trump. *Cagle*. https://www.cagle.com/jd-crowe/2020/07/the-taliban-putin-and-trump

Cummings, W. (2020, June 29). Reports say Russia offered bounty on US troops in Afghanistan. Here's what we know. *USA Today*. https://www.usatoday.com/story/news/politics/2020/06/29/russia-bounty-us-troops-afghanistan-what-we-know/3277696001/

Donovan-Smith, O. (2020, November 2). Whether Trump or Biden wins, the U.S. will have its oldest president ever; should that matter? https://www.spokesman.com/stories/2020/nov/02/whether-trump-or-biden-wins-the-us-will-have-its-o/

Edwards, J. L. (1997). *Political cartoons in the 1988 presidential campaign: Image, metaphor, and narrative.* Garland.

Edwards, J. L., & Winkler, C. K. (1997). Representative form and the visual ideograph: The Iwo Jima image in editorial cartoons. *Quarterly Journal of Speech, 83,* 289–310.

Esquivel, A. (2018). Latest cartoons. *The Week*. https://theweek.com/cartoons/839905/political-cartoon-trump-lies-pinocchio

Fitzsimmons, D. (2019). Latest cartoons. *The Week*. https://theweek.com/cartoons/833107/political-cartoon-joe-biden-metoo-misconduct-allegations

Frantzich, S. (2020, September 10). Joe Biden has a history of gaffes, but what do they mean? | *Commentary*. https://www.baltimoresun.com/opinion/op-ed/bs-ed-op-0913-joe-biden-gaffes-20200910-nfcd3z575rfn3cijxkzosa2k6y-story.html

Feng, D., & O'Halloran, K. L. (2013). The visual representation of metaphor: A social semiotic approach. *Review of Cognitive Linguistics, 11,* 320–335.

Hands, P. (2020a, March 8). Hands on Wisconsin: Joe Biden and Bernie Sanders are the grumpiest old men. *The Wisconsin State Journal*. https://madison.com/opinion/cartoon/hands-on-wisconsin-joe-biden-and-bernie-sanders-are-the-grumpiest-old-men/article_0aed77a6-92eb-5a02-abb2-bcfe8d522574.html

Hands, P. (2020b, March 2). Hands on Wisconsin: Creepy uncle joe gets a key endorsement. *The Wisconsin State Journal*. https://madison.com/opinion/cartoon/hands-on-wiscon

sin-creepy-uncle-joe-gets-a-key-endorsement/article_2fff904a-ed63-5a3a-989c-a3705
968245c.html

Horsey, D. (2020, July 2). The week in cartons: June 29–July 3. *U.S. News & World Report.*
https://www.usnews.com/news/cartoons/2020/06/29/the-coronavirus-face-masks-and-
president-donald-trump-the-week-in-cartoons-for-june-29-july-3

Jones, T. (2012, April 27). Five funny Biden gaffe cartoons. *NBC News.* https://www.nbcnews.
com/news/world/five-funny-biden-gaffe-cartoons-flna738660

Kelley-Roman, S., & Westgate, V. (2007). Blaming Bush: An analysis of political cartoons
following Hurricane Katrina. *Journalism Studies, 8*, 755–773.

Luckovich, M. (2019). Latest cartoons. *The Week.* https://theweek.com/cartoons/883348/politi
cal-cartoon-trump-flushed-truth-down-toilet

MacGregor, D. (2018). August political cartoons from the USA Today Network. *USA Today.*
https://www.usatoday.com/picture-gallery/opinion/nation-now/2018/08/01/august-politi
cal-cartoons-usa-today-network/861864002/

McCaskill, N. D. (2016, October 19). Gingrich: Little Trump reacts to criticism 'almost uncontrollably'. *Politico.* https://www.politico.com/story/2016/10/newt-gingrich-trump-reacts-
almost-uncontrollably-229978.

McGee, M. C. (1980). The ideograph: A link between rhetoric and ideology. *Quarterly Journal
of Speech, 66*, 1–16.

McKee, R. (2019, August 20). Biden podium. *Cagle.* https://www.cagle.com/rick-mckee/2019/
08/biden-podium

Medhurst, M. J., & DeSousa, M. A. (1981). Political cartoons as rhetorical form: A taxonomy
of graphic discourse. *Communication Monographs, 48*, 197–236.

Morris, J. S. (2009). *The Daily Show with Jon Stewart* and audience attitude change during the
2004 party conventions. *Political Behavior, 31*, 79–102.

Morrison, M. C. (1969). The role of the political cartoonist in image making. *Central States
Speech Journal, 20*, 252–260.

Ortiz, J. L. (2021, January 17). 400,000 COVID-19 deaths, experts blame Trump administration for a 'preventable' loss of life. *USA Today.* https://www.usatoday.com/story/news/
nation/2021/01/17/covid-19-us-400-000-deaths-experts-blame-trump-administration/664
2685002/

Satija, N. (2019, June 5). Echoes of Biden's 1987 plagiarism scandal continue to reverberate.
*Washington Post.* https://www.washingtonpost.com/investigations/echoes-of-bidens-1987-
plagiarism-scandal-continue-to-reverberate/2019/06/05/dbaf3716-7292-11e9-9eb4-082
8f5389013_story.html

Streicher, L. H. (1965). David Low and the sociology of caricature. *Comparative Studies in
Society and History, 8*, 1–23.

Stiglich, T. (2019, April 7). Joe Biden is the least of the democrat's problems: Political cartoons.
*Los Angeles Daily News.* https://www.dailynews.com/2019/04/07/joe-biden-is-the-least-of-
the-democrats-problem-political-cartoons/

Sutton, (2020, September 11). Grave consequences. *The Boston Globe.* https://www.bostongl
obe.com/2020/09/11/opinion/grave-consequences/

Thibodeau, R. (1989). From racism to tokenism: The changing face of blacks in New Yorker cartoons. *Public Opinion Quarterly, 53*, 482–494.

Tillett, E. (2019, April 3). Pro-Trump PAC releases "creepy Joe" ad in the wake of Biden allegations. *CBS News*. https://www.cbsnews.com/news/pro-trump-pac-releases-creepy-joe-ad-in-wake-of-bidens-inappropriate-behavior-allegations/

Trump tells Woodward he deliberatively downplayed coronavirus threat. (2020, September 10). *NPR*. https://www.npr.org/2020/09/10/911368698/trump-tells-woodward-he-deliberately-downplayed-coronavirus-threat

Verhulsdonk, I., Nai, A., & Karp, J. (2022). Are political attacks a laughing matter? Three experiments on political humor and the effectiveness of negative campaigning. *Political Research Quarterly, 75*, 720–737.

Walters, K. (2020, October 7). Grumpy old men cartoon. *Trinity Journal*. www.trinityjournal.com/opinion/cartoons/image_048a487e-0824-11eb-ab38-37978fa91d29.html

Weyant, C. (2020, July 2). Off target. *The Boston Globe*. https://www.bostonglobe.com/2020/07/02/opinion/off-target/

Whamond, D. (2020a). Coronavirus cartoons: Trump sees ratings bump amid record job losses, stock drops. *The Mercury News*. https://www.mercurynews.com/2020/03/31/coronavirus-cartoons-trump-sees-ratings-bump-amid-record-job-losses-stock-drops/

Whamond, D. (2020b). The best editorial cartoons of 2020: Volume 1. *HeraldNet*. https://www.heraldnet.com/opinion/the-best-editorial-cartoons-of-2020-volume-1/

Wiid, R., Pitt, L. F., & Engstrom, A. (2011). Not so sexy: Public opinion of political sex scandals as reflected in political cartoons. *Journal of Public Affairs, 11*, 137–147.

Zyglist, A. (2020, March 12). Adam Zyglist: COVID-19 leadership. *Buffalo News*. https://buffalonews.com/opinion/adam-zyglis-covid-19-leadership/article_0c7beac0-949c-565d-842b-f74f2cc4358c.html

# · 8 ·

# PERSUASIVE ATTACK IN 2020 PRESIDENTIAL AND VICE PRESIDENTIAL DEBATES

Televised campaign debates are an established component of political campaigns; these messages rely frequently on attacks (Benoit, 2014a,b, 2022). This chapter offers a deeper dive into the nature of attacks in presidential campaign messages. The 2020 presidential election was heated, perhaps even more heated than usual. The divide between Democrats and Republicans was extremely wide. The disparity in the approval rate of President Donald Trump, who was seeking a second term in office, was 89% (Jones, 2020). Former Senator and Vice President Joe Biden was the Democratic nominee. He faced a business magnate, a former television personality, and President Donald Trump, who represented the GOP as the incumbent. The presidential candidates faced off at Case Western Reserve University in Cleveland on September 29, 2020, and at Belmont University in Nashville on October 22, 2020. The October 15, 2020 presidential debate had been canceled after President Trump was hospitalized for a COVID-19 infection and the Trump campaign refused to participate in a virtual debate. The vice presidential candidates (Democratic Senator Kamala Harris and Republican former governor and Vice President Mike Pence) met at the University of Utah in Salt Lake City on October 7, 2020.

Research using the Functional Theory of Political Campaign Discourse has documented the frequent occurrence of persuasive attacks in presidential debates. Research on previous presidential debates found that attacks comprised 36% of utterances in previous presidential debates (1960, 1976–2016) and 41 percent of statements in vice presidential debates (1976, 1984–2016) (Benoit, 2014a; Benoit & Glantz, 2020). The frequency of these utterances in debates means that the presidential and vice presidential debates of 2020 should be an appropriate place for an exploratory study of the Theory of Persuasive Attack.

## Attacks in the 2020 Debates

Analysis of these two debates reveals that these four candidates did use strategies to intensify their attacks in these texts. Note that the Theory of Persuasive Attack does not assert that attackers should employ any particular strategy, a particular combination of strategies, or that more strategies are necessarily better than fewer strategies. This is an exploratory study to see whether, and if so, how, presidential campaign debates use these strategies.

## Attacks on Behavior

First, these candidates in these texts used strategies to enhance attacks on behavior (or policy) more than attacks on character (87% to 13%). For example, Biden criticized the president over his handling of the COVID-19 pandemic, lamenting "the 200,000 people that have died on his watch." Trump replied in kind, declaring that Biden "had 308,000 military people die because you couldn't provide them proper care in the military." Both of these excerpts intensify the attack by pointing to the extent of the problem and stressing offensiveness (all excerpts taken from the presidential debate can be found in "Transcript," 2020).

Strategies for enhancing persuasive attack also occurred at the vice presidential event. Harris argued that Pence (and Trump) knew about the coronavirus in January, emphasizing their blame for this crisis: "The vice president is the head of the task force and knew, on January 29, how serious this was." She also attacked Trump and Pence for rushing to fill Ruth Bader Ginsburg's Supreme Court seat before the election: "Abraham Lincoln was up for reelection, and it was 27 days before the election and a seat became open on the

United States Supreme Court. But Honest Abe said it's not the right thing to do." This statement uses guilt by contrast to attack her opponents (and perhaps also implies a contrast between Trump and the Republican icon, "Honest Abe" Lincoln, on grounds of honesty). Pence stressed offensiveness by criticizing the Democrats' Green New Deal, arguing that it "would increase the energy cost of American families in their home" (all excerpts from this debate can be found in Page, 2020). Historically, using the Functional Theory of Political Campaign Discourse, presidential and vice presidential debates also stressed policy over character across both acclaim and attacks, but the disparity is less lopsided (70% policy to 30% character; Benoit, 2014a; Benoit & Glantz, 2020) than for strategies of persuasive attack (Table 8.1).

As explained earlier, a persuasive attack is comprised of two elements: offensiveness and blame. We can also determine the relative emphasis of these elements of attack. In these texts, 79% of the strategies were used to intensify offensiveness (of behavior or of a trait), whereas 21% addressed blame (or possession of a character trait). For example, Biden intensified offensive behavior with attacks highlighting the effects of this disease on the victims (direct and indirect) of the coronavirus: "How many of you got up this morning and had an empty chair at the kitchen table because someone died of COVID? How many of you … lost your mom or dad and couldn't even speak to the nurse holding the phone up so you could in fact say goodbye?" This statement highlights the effects of the COVID-19 pandemic on the families of victims. Trump, on the other hand, criticized the Obama–Biden administration for a slow economic recovery: "They had the slowest recovery … since 1929." This remark implies that the Democratic plan for economic recovery was deeply flawed. Together, these two excerpts address the offensiveness of actions attributed to their opponents.

## Attacks on Character

In the vice presidential debate, Harris brought up allegations that Russia had put bounties on American soldiers in Afghanistan: "Donald Trump has talked at least six times to Vladimir Putin and never brought up the subject." The argument here is that the president was clearly to blame because he repeatedly refused to confront Putin (his failure to do so was no accident or simple oversight). Pence criticized Biden for his handling of the swine flu outbreak in 2009. Biden's Chief of Staff, Ron Klain, said that Obama and Biden did

**Table 8.1.** Strategies for Intensifying Attacks in 2020 Presidential and Vice Presidential Debates

| | Presidential | Vice Presidential |
|---|---|---|
| **Intensifying Attacks on Actions** | | |
| *Perceived Responsibility for Act (Belief)* | | |
| Committed the Act Repeatedly | 0 | 3 |
| Planned the Act | 0 | 0 |
| Knew Consequences (or Knew about Problem) | 3 | 3 |
| Benefitted from Act | 0 | 0 |
| Blame Subtotal | 6 | 6 |
| *Negative Perceptions of Act (Value)* | | |
| Extent of Harms | 50 | 25 |
| Persistence of Effects | 0 | 0 |
| Effects on Victims | 7 | 13 |
| Inconsistency | 0 | 0 |
| Victims of Acts | 0 | 0 |
| Obligation to Protect Victims | 0 | 0 |
| Offensiveness Subtotal | 57 | 38 |
| Total Attacks on Behavior | 63 | 44 |
| **Intensifying Attacks on Character** | | |
| *Target Possesses Trait (Belief)* | | |
| Extent of Trait | 4 | 9 |
| Performed Acts Consistent with Trait | 0 | 0 |
| Made Statements Consistent with Trait | 0 | 0 |
| Associates with Unsavory People | 0 | 0 |
| Accused Contrasted with Respected People | 0 | 1 |
| Blame Subtotal | 4 | 10 |
| *Trait is Offensive (Value)* | | |
| Particularly Repulsive Example of Trait | 1 | 1 |

Table 8.1. Continued

|  | Presidential | Vice Presidential |
|---|---|---|
| People Negatively Affected by Trait | 0 | 0 |
| Offensiveness Subtotal | 1 | 1 |
| Total Attacks on Character | 5 | 11 |

action vs. character: $\chi^2$ ($df$=1) = 67.33, $p$<.0001.

blame vs. offensiveness: $\chi^2$ ($df$=1) = 40.98, $p$<.0001.

"everything possible wrong," and only luck prevented more deaths. This statement suggests that the Democrats did not make a single mistake, but they were wrong in every way due to deficiencies of character.

## Observations and Conclusions

This analysis investigates the use of strategies for persuasive attack in political campaign debates. This exploratory study suggests that presidential candidates may be more likely to intensify their attacks using strategies for enhancing offensiveness more often than blame, although strategies to elaborate both elements of persuasive attack occurred in these texts. One explanation for this difference is that Biden's camp assumes the audience is already likely to assign responsibility to President Trump, so all they need to do is ratchet up the attacks on the severity of the problem (e.g., COVID deaths) to develop a complete attack. However, the risk of this strategy is that audiences may believe multiple political actors or organizations share a role in addressing the problem. In that way, only establishing severity does not necessarily make the problem Trump's fault, but it does make for a more well-rounded attack.

Although the numbers show a proclivity toward policy, statistically speaking, it is nearly impossible to clearly separate out the policy and character statements. For example, when Biden argues that Trump severely mishandled the COVID-19 crisis, he is also indirectly arguing that everything Trump said previously, touting his record on COVID, was fabricated, misleading, or an outright lie (Benoit & Stein, 2022). Thus, not only are his policies under attack, but his character is clearly flawed. Conversely, when Trump argues that Obama and Biden dropped the ball on their handling of the swine flu crisis, he is not only criticizing their policy decisions but also their inability to competently respond to a crisis, especially one that reached beyond national borders.

Both topics of campaign discourse were addressed in these attacks; still, these messages were prone to enhance attacks on policy (behavior) more so than character (personality). Table 8.1 shows the variety of strategies employed in these texts for enhancing both offensiveness and blame. Even though Benoit establishes that a complete attack should establish responsibility and offensiveness, statements in those two areas do not always have to be explicitly articulated. Sometimes, the audience will assign responsibility or offensiveness on their own, and, therefore, the attacker only has to fill in the gaps. In a way, this relationship operates on a simple enthymematic level where the major and minor premises are supplied so believably that the audience can easily draw its own conclusion. This also holds true with attackers only articulating the behavioral piece and not the character piece. The audience will usually connect those two naturally.

# References

Benoit, W. L. (2014a). *Political election debates: Informing voters about policy and character.* Lexington Books.

Benoit, W. L. (2014b). *Seeing spots: A functional analysis of presidential television advertisements from 1952–2012* (2nd ed). Lexington Books.

Benoit, W. L. (2022). *Communication in political campaigns: Functional analysis of election messages* (2nd ed.). Peter Lang.

Benoit, W. L., & Glantz, M. (2020). *Presidential campaigns in the age of social media: Clinton and Trump.* Peter Lang.

Benoit, W. L., & Stein, K. A. (2022). 2020 Presidential Debates: The Coronavirus clash. *Speaker & Gavel, 58*(1), 8–31.

Jones, J. M. (2020, July 6). Trump's job approval rating steady at lower level. *Gallup.* https://news.gallup.com/poll/313454/trump-job-approval-rating-steady-lower-level.aspx

Page, S. (2020, October 8). Read the full transcript of vice presidential debate between Mike Pence and Kamala Harris. *USA Today.* https://www.usatoday.com/story/news/politics/elections/2020/10/08/vice-presidential-debate-full-transcript-mike-pence-and-kamala-harris/5920773002/

Transcript from the first presidential debate between Joe Biden and Donald Trump. (2020, September 30). *USA Today.* https://www.usatoday.com/story/news/politics/elections/2020/09/30/presidential-debate-read-full-transcript-first-debate/3587462001/

# · 9 ·

# CICERO'S PERSUASIVE ATTACK IN THE
# *VERRINE ORATIONS*

The Roman Gaius Verres served first as *quaestor* (the official in charge of an army's treasury) for Gnaeus Carbo in 84 B.C.E., and then as *legatus* (general of an army) for Gnaeus Cornelius Dolabella in 81 B.C.E. Next, he served as a *praetor* (a Roman official second only in rank to Consul); his duties in this position were judicial. He bribed his way into the governorship (*propraetor*) of Sicily in 74 B.C.E., where he plundered citizens, farmers (Sicily supplied huge amounts of grain to Rome), and temples.

Cicero was born in Arpinum but moved to Rome to pursue a public career in law. Marcus Tullius Cicero announced his intention to prosecute Verres for his actions upon the latter's return to Rome in 70 B.C.E. One of Verres' cronies, Quintus Caecilius Niger, volunteered to prosecute the defendant; Cicero gave a speech arguing that he, rather than Niger, should be the one to prosecute. Cicero was chosen to be the prosecutor, and the renowned Roman advocate Quintus Hortensius agreed to defend Verres ("Speech Delivered Against Quintus Caecilius Niger"). At that point in time, Cicero was nearing the beginning of his career in Rome, while Hortensius stood at the pinnacle of his profession.

Cicero prepared several speeches in his prosecution of Verres. His first speech against Verres as a prosecutor outlined his case; along with his anticipatory speeches, this discourse was collected in the corpus of the "Verrine Orations" and was written as responses to Hortensius' anticipated defense. However, Cicero's first speech attacking Verres was so powerful that Hortensius refused to mount a response and advised Verres to go into exile. The defendant decided to flee to Massilia (present-day Marseille) rather than allow Cicero more opportunities to attack him. Verres' concession meant that Cicero's additional prepared attacks were not needed in the trial; still, Cicero published the remaining material to adorn his rising reputation as an advocate. His persuasive attack against Gaius Verres is very important for three reasons: (1) it ended Verres' career; (2) it provided a sense of justice to the people in Sicily; and (3) most importantly, it firmly established Cicero's career in Rome. Less than 10 years later, Cicero would be elected Consul, the highest-ranking magistrate of Rome. Cicero leveled a multitude of accusations against the defendant. This chapter will investigate the persuasive attack by Cicero on Verres.

## Cicero's Persuasive Attack Against Verres

The prosecutor in this case argued that Verres' wrongdoing did not consist of isolated actions but was a consistent (repeated) pattern of misbehavior when he said that "Verres never let one minute go by without doing something wrong" (p.233). Cicero (1928) made it clear the extent of the defendant's pillaging:

> Verres did not leave one single statue behind; that from temples and public places alike, with the whole of Aspendus looking on, they were all openly loaded on wagons and carted away. Yes, even the famous [statue of the] Harper of Aspendus ... him too Verres carried off and put right inside his own house. (p.177)

Cicero also declared that "the behavior of Verres, at every state of his journey, made him seem less like a Roman governor than a kind of human pestilence" (pp. 167–168), harsh words indicating the extent of Verres' villainy. Cicero averred that Verres's "term of service as adjutant was a disaster to the whole of the provinces of Asia (Asia Province is part of present day Turkey) and Pamphylia (an area in Asia Minor), where few private houses, very few cities, and not one sanctuary escaped his depredations" (pp. 78–79). This statement indicated the effects of Verres' crimes on his victims, thereby demonstrating that perpetrating a "disaster" is particularly offensive. Similarly, Cicero accused

Verres of "the spoliation of our friends and allies" (p.181). Committing these acts against any victims would be bad enough; the fact that Verres' victims were friends and allies of Rome increased the offensiveness of these misdeeds.

The defendant was accused of wrongful acts throughout his career as a Roman official, but Cicero argued: "nowhere did he multiply and magnify the memorials and the proofs of all his evil qualities so thoroughly as in his governorship of Sicily, which island for the space of three years he devastated and ruined so effectively that nothing can restore to its former condition" (p.79). This argument stressed the extent of the accused's misdeeds, characterizing his actions as causing "devastation" and "ruin." Cicero asked, "Ah, Verres, how many there are to whom your praetership has brought pain and misery and shame?" (p.269). Similarly, Cicero declared that Verres' "career [is] convicted already of countless vices and countless crimes, and condemned long ago by the feelings, and by the judgment, of all the world" (p.77). The prosecutor also identified the effects of Verres' actions on the audience, declaring, "By your vile and wicked conduct you have defiled the fair name of Roman government in the eyes of all foreign nations" (p.209). This characterization surely would not have pleased the jury.

## Verres' Theft and Graft

One of the five specific attacks investigated here is the accusation of theft and graft. Cicero argued that Verres' depredations began in the very first public office he held: "The moment he saw his chance – note the man's first step as a public official and administrator – this precious *quaestor* embezzled the public money, and deserted his consul, his consul's army, and his sacred duty" (p.159). Verres' string of offensive acts began as soon as he launched his public career. The prosecutor argued that Verres' avarice continued unrelentingly throughout his career and was extensive indeed: "He has robbed the Treasury, and plundered Asia [Turkey] and Pamphylia; he has behaved like a pirate in his city praetorship, and like a destroying pestilence in his province of Sicily" (p.71). Robbery and plundering are offensive acts; being called a "pirate" and a "pestilence" are far from terms of endearment. The prosecutor explained that as soon as he became governor of Sicily, before leaving Rome, he began to "ask himself, and to discuss with his friends, by what methods he could make the most money" out of his province (p.311). In other words, Verres planned his program of theft and graft. Cicero said that Verres committed offensive acts continuously: "Not one hour, it will be found, has been free from robbery and crime, from cruelty and wickedness" (p.157). The extent of Verres' misdeeds is huge. The orator from Arpinum listed multiple acts of graft and theft perpetrated by the accused:

> Countless sums of money, under a new and unprincipled regulation, were wrung from the purses of the farmers ... the guiltiest criminals bought their legal acquittal ... Famous and ancient works of art, some of them gifts of wealthy kings, who intended them to adorn the cities where they stood, others the gifts of Roman generals, who gave or restored them to the communities of Sicily in the hour of victory – this same governor stripped and despoiled every one of them. (p.81)

This passage manages to make use of multiple strategies for intensifying the attack: repeated and extensive offenses (e.g., plundering "countless sums of money" and "famous and ancient works of art") were perpetrated by the accused. Verres' incredible avarice was described in Cicero's attack.

One of Verres's extortion schemes functioned by "demanding corn [from residents] and making them pay money instead" (p.223). This way, Verres did not have to bother with selling the grain he requisitioned; the victims of his extortion simply gave him money directly. Cicero made it clear that this kind of extortion was conducted "throughout Lycia and Pamphylia, Pisidia and Phrygia" (p.223). This attack made it clear that this form of theft was not an isolated instance but a repeated pattern of misbehavior. Furthermore, Cicero firmly fixed the blame on the defendant: "It was all carried out under Verres' personal direction" (p.225). The prosecutor declared that "It was you, Verres, I assert, who made these requisitions, you who fixed their value in money, you to whom the money was paid" (p.225). This attack explicitly argued that Verres planned these repeated and extensive offensive actions.

## Verres Pillaged Temples

Cicero reported that Verres plundered a multitude of temples. These accusations are a variation on the strategy of intensifying negative perceptions of the act by arguing that victims are innocent or helpless. Verres did not simply steal from people, which is offensive enough; he stole from *temples*. Cicero explained that the defendant "has despoiled sanctuaries" (p.131). The man from Arpinum added that Verres "pillaged the holiest and most venerated sanctuaries; in fact, he has left not the people of Sicily a single god whose workmanship he thought at all above the average of artistic merit" (p.81).

This statement indicated the extent of Verres' vile acts committed against temples in Sicily.

Cicero also named several specific temples in his attack. For example, "At Athens a large amount of gold was carried away from the temple of Minerva ... Verres did not merely take part: He took command" (p.169). Notice that the assertion that Verres "took command" of this pillaging indicates his responsibility for this act. Furthermore, the prosecutor related that to Delos "one night he secretly carried off, from the much-revered sanctuary of Apollo, several ancient and beautiful statues" (p.169). Cicero declared, "You dared to rob Apollo – Apollo of Delos! Upon that temple, so ancient, so holy, so profoundly venerated, you sought to lay your impious and sacrilegious hands?" (p.171). This action was far more offensive than simple theft; Cicero characterized it explicitly as sacrilege.

The prosecutor added yet another temple robbed by Verres: "At Perga there is, as we know, a much revered sanctuary of Diana; I assert that this too has been stripped and plundered by him, and that all the fold from the figure of Diana herself has been pulled off and taken away" (p.177). The persuasive attack also explicitly argued that this kind of theft from temples was an offensive act repeatedly committed by the accused: "He carried off statues of great beauty from Chios, and also from Erythrae and Halicarnassus." From Tenes, god of Tenedos, a beautiful work of art "he carried off, amid the loud lamentations of the citizens. And then mark how he stormed and sacked the ancient and glorious temple of Juno of Samos" (p.173).

Cicero also employs the strategy of emphasizing the extent of damage in connection with Verres' sacking of temples: "Was ever such devouring greed known before, greed capable of such destruction of what is high and holy?" (p.173). Cicero pointed to Syracuse (a large city in Sicily), declaring that "the whole city was stripped of its treasures ... he carried off from the temples in the city every statue, every ivory carving, every painting, and every sacred image on which he chose to lay his hands" (p.349). This was an astounding act of theft by Verres. Cicero characterized Verres as a sacrilegious monster who repeatedly despoiled temples. This criticism links the accusation of theft or graft generally and the robbery of temples specifically through a common thread—Verres' exceptional greed.

## Verres' Cruelty

This attack excoriated Verres for his extreme cruelty. Cicero related to the jury that "Marcus Annius ... stated that, in his presence, a Roman citizen was beheaded" (p.135). Similarly, the prosecutor stated that "The knight Lucius Flavius ... has given evidence on oath that his acquaintance Herennius, a banker from Africa, was beheaded at Syracuse" (p.135). To establish the extent of Verres' cruelty, Cicero lamented that the defendant had "butchered a multitude of innocent persons, slain and tortured and crucified citizens of Rome" (p.131). No one should ever be butchered, but this act appeared even more savage when the jury heard that the victims were innocent citizens of Rome. The Roman jury was likely moved by this accusation. Furthermore, the prosecutor declared that "Lucius Suettius ... has testified an oath before you to the cruel and violent death inflicted on many Roman citizens in the stone quarries by Verres' orders" (p.135). Cicero lamented the fact that "Roman citizens were tortured and executed like slaves" (p.81). Torture and execution confirm Verres' extreme cruelty. The fact that many of Verres' victims were Roman citizens was likely to make these deaths appear more vile in the eyes of jurors, another incarnation of the idea that an offense appears particularly heinous. This statement confirms the extent of Verres' killings.

Cicero also related cruelties perpetrated by Verres that stopped short of death. For example, in Achaia, Verres,

> ... demanded a sum of money from the chief magistrate of Sicyon ...The magistrate refusing, Verres punished him ... He ordered a fire of moist green wood to be made in a confined spot: And there this free-born man, a man of high rank in his own town, one of the allies and friends of Rome, was put through the agonies of suffocation, and left there more dead than alive. (p.169)

This persuasive attack portrayed Verres as a vicious and barbaric thug. Cicero also related the fact that "Sicilian soldiers and sailors, our allies and our friends, were starved to death" (p. 81). Cicero argued strenuously that Verres was an extremely cruel person.

## Verres' Low Moral Character

Cicero pretended to pass over some of Verres' faults. By simply mentioning these criticisms without elaboration, he attacks Verres' character:

I shall ... pass over the notoriously vile and immoral "first act" of Verres' career. He shall hear nothing from me of the sins of his boyhood, no tales of his unclean ... I shall pass over all that I cannot refer to without indecency ... Please allow me the liberty of holding my tongue about some small part of his shameless career. (p.155)

Cicero used this approach elsewhere in his attack, mentioning alleged offenses without elaborating on them: "Let nothing be said about his drunken orgies that lasted all night; let there be no mention of pimps and gamblers and seducers; let his inroads on his father's purse and his defilements of his own manhood, be passed by without a word" (p.157). The prosecutor pretends to overlook some of Verres' misdeeds out of concern for his victims:

As to his adulteries and the like vile offenses, a sense of decency makes me afraid to repeat the tale of his acts of wanton wickedness; and besides, I would not wish, by repeating it, to add to the calamities of those who have not been suffered to save their children and their wives from outrage at the hands of this lecherous scoundrel. (pp. 81–82)

Cicero's attack worked to vilify his target's character while adopting the pose that he would not rake up salacious accusations against Verres (when he clearly mentioned these criticisms). This approach may also allow the prosecutor to slander the defendant without providing evidence. After all, he declared that he would "pass over" these accusations.

## Verres' Actions as Judge

A final accusation examined here is an attack on Verres' actions as a judge. Cicero repeatedly accused Verres of inconsistency in his judicial decisions. He lamented "the lack of uniformity in his decisions" (p.251). Cicero indicated that Verres was random in his issuance of decrees: "He would, without the least scruple, deliver in one case a judgement directly opposed to that which he had delivered in the previous case a few minutes before" (p.253). This inconsistency was committed over and over (repeated offenses): "Lucius Piso filled a pile of notebooks with records of the cases in which he vetoed decisions by Verres as inconsistent with Verres' own edict" (p.251). His inconsistencies included altering verdicts he had already handed down. After he issued a trial verdict, when one of the parties "came up to him and whispered in his ear, he would call back the parties to a case that he had already judged, and alter his judgement" (p.251). Reversing his own judgment is blatantly inconsistent and, therefore, offensive. Cicero also argued that Verres benefitted from his decisions, taking bribes for favorable verdicts: "He did not hesitate to demand a bribe in return for his decision in court" (p.261).

Another attack combined the strategies of extent and benefit: "I could produce hundreds of his decisions whose disregard for precedent and equity makes it plain ... that money has had a hand in them" (p.257). Verres' "misdeeds of this kind [judicial] are without number" (p.419), an argument for the extent of his offensive actions. Cicero attacked the quality of Verres' judicial decisions, their inconsistency, and the fact that he benefited from these decisions by soliciting bribes. Notice that the allegation that Verres' taking bribes arose from his greed. Several of these accusations in this persuasive attack tend to support each other.

## Observations and Conclusions

Cicero advanced a multitude of attacks on Gaius Verres in the *Verrine Orations*, five of which are investigated here. This speech illustrated how an attack can intensify the offensiveness of the wrongdoing through several strategies (extent of the damage, repeated misdeeds, effects on victims, victims were innocent (people and structures), and their targeting was particularly offensive, and inconsistency). Cicero also exemplified the way attacks can address blame by stressing the claim that Verres was responsible for these misdeeds (planned the act, benefited from the act). It is understandable that Hortensius, the defense attorney in this case, chose not to defend Verres and instead advised him to admit to the accusations and go into voluntary exile. This decision allowed Verres to retain some of his property that would have been seized if he had lost the case).

We identified in these texts a new variant of the strategy that victims are innocent or helpless: thefts from temples are more heinous than other thefts. We also saw that several of these accusations supported one another by pointing to a common motivating factor: greed. Once an audience member accepts that the accused was filled with greed based on one accusation, that person is likely to accept other accusations based on greed. Establishing a motive behind an act creates a lens for guilt that is both widely accepted and not easily ignored. It is like the contemporary jury, who is more likely to assign guilt by asking the question, "Why would this person commit this act without a compelling reason?" At times, a behavioral motive may be falsely assigned or even acknowledged in a way that tempers a particular act, but more often than not, once a motive is assigned and paired with distasteful treatment of a vulnerable population, the behavior can be seen as avoidable or unnecessary by the audience.

Finally, we thought it was interesting, and probably effective, to slander the target while pretending to skip over alleged flaws. In other words, this chapter is a reminder of the fallacy of paralepsis, wherein the attacker mentions character deficiencies without elaborating on them, claiming that more detail would cause them to lower their own moral standards. This move fuels the attack in a more subtle way when detailed and vague attacks appear to assert the same level of impact on the target.

# Reference

Cicero. (1928). *The Verrine Orations*, Volume I: Against Caecilius. Against Verres, Part 1; Part 2, Books 1–2. Trans. L. H. G. Greenwood. Loeb Classical Library 221. Harvard University Press.

# Part IV
## SOCIAL ISSUES

# · 1 0 ·

# THE COWARD FROM BROWARD: A PERSUASIVE ATTACK ON DEPUTY SCOT PETERSON FOLLOWING THE PARKLAND SHOOTING

On February 14, 2018, a gunman opened fire with an AR-15-style semi-automatic rifle at Marjory Stoneman Douglas High School in Parkland, Florida. The shooter, Nikolas Cruz, a 19-year-old formerly expelled student, systematically worked his way through three floors of the school's Building 12, killing 17 people and injuring 17 others (Chuck et al., 2018). He attempted to maximize the number of deaths by triggering the fire alarm in order to move people out into the open hallways of the building. Cruz faced little resistance from the unarmed students, but beloved assistant football coach and school security guard Aaron Feis ran into the building and gave his own life as he shielded several students from the gunfire (Dusenbury, 2018). All in all, the violent rampage lasted six minutes before Cruz left the building and headed off campus on foot. He was apprehended a little over an hour later by police after being spotted by an officer on the lookout for someone of Cruz's description (Chavez, 2018a).

Feiss' heroic actions stood in stark contrast to 56-year-old school resource deputy Scot Peterson, who became embroiled in controversy after video surveillance was released showing him approach Building 12 with a pistol in hand, yet never entered the building for the duration of the shooting. Once a Broward County Sheriff's deputy, Peterson was trained to "interrupt a shooting and search for victims when there's a ceasefire" (Chavez, 2018b). The video, at least to most observers, seemed to show Peterson doing just the opposite. Naturally, other members of law enforcement, the parents of the children killed, and members of the general public were incensed over the idea that an armed officer could have intervened to save the lives of innocent children and failed to act. Broward County Sheriff Scott Israel described what he saw in the video surveillance of Peterson at the scene of the shooting: "What I saw was a deputy arrive at the west side of Building 12, take up a position, and he never went in" ("Broward Sheriff, 2018). Fred Guttenberg, whose daughter Jaime was among the victims, attacked Peterson, saying "I'm sorry, but he failed. He failed our children and they're gone" (Bacon, 2018). Even President Donald Trump weighed in on the controversy: "When it came time to get in there and do something, he didn't have the courage or something happened, but he certainly did a poor job. There's no question about that. He didn't turn out to be too good, I'll tell you that. Turned out to be not good, not a credit to law enforcement, I can tell you that" (Stracqualursi, 2018). Although the origins of the moniker are unclear, the nickname "Coward from Broward" emerged in media coverage across the country (Hassan, 2019).

This particular case is a noteworthy example of an attack for several reasons: (1) Most cases focus on perpetrated harmful behaviors. This one is an attack stemming from a lack of action. It was a failure to do something good rather than the act of doing something harmful; (2) The case is a good context for examining character attacks since it became questionable whether he actually did something illegal. Although prosecutors charged him with child neglect, many legal experts wondered if the charges would stick since "first responders" had never been charged with failure to act before and the child neglect standard is a broad brush with which to paint Scot Peterson; (3) Attacks were coming from numerous directions, such as parents, students, law enforcement officers, politicians, and media commentators; (4) The tragedy occupies a space as the most violent high school shooting in history and in the top 10 of mass shootings in US history.

## Strategies of Persuasive Attack Against Scot Peterson

The primary public attacks on Scot Peterson came from then Broward County Sheriff Scott Israel, the parents of many of the victims, and then President

Donald Trump. Primary sources were transcribed and analyzed when available, but secondary sources, such as newspaper articles containing quotes, were also used when necessary. The primary attacks focused on the following: (1) Scot Peterson was derelict in his sworn duty to protect the students; (2) Peterson's inaction caused innocent victims to be killed; (3) Peterson did not act because he was a coward and unmotivated to act; and (4) Peterson attempted to portray himself as a victim.

## Scot Peterson's Dereliction of Duty

Only one strategy was used to increase Peterson's level of responsibility, and that was to argue that he planned the act. His accusers did not suggest that an extensive level of forethought went into his decision to remain paralyzed during the shooting, but some argued that there was intentionality behind his decision. For example, Sheriff Scott Israel, in a statement released through his attorney, said: "This was something that is not surprising. We believe now that FDLE [Florida Department of Law Enforcement] took the time and conducted 184 witness interviews and prepared statements and came to the same conclusion that this was the intentional inaction of Scot Peterson that caused those injuries to adults and children" (Susskind & Rodriguez, 2019). Israel's statement asserts that Peterson knew he was supposed to intervene on behalf of the children and that his actions represented the willful neglect of the students at Marjory Stoneman Douglas High School.

In addition to attacks designed to increase responsibility, some were levied with the goal of increasing the offensiveness of Peterson's actions. These include arguments suggesting that he had an obligation to protect victims. Sheriff Scott Israel criticized Peterson during his interview with *CNN*'s Jake Tapper: "We'll get to the truth, but at this point one deputy was remiss. Dereliction of duty and he's no longer with this agency" (CNN, 2018). In another example, Fred Guttenberg (the father of Jaime Guttenberg) argued: "He keeps mentioning the third floor. If he had done his job, this killing wouldn't have made it to the third floor. Those people who lost their lives, including my daughter, are victims of his inability to do his job; victims of his failure" (Miller & Madan, 2018). Similarly, Andrew Pollock (the father of Meadow Pollock) blasted Peterson for his failure: "I think the whole country knows he didn't do his job and this interview was his way of him trying to live with it ... He could have stopped it. Could have saved my kid. Nobody should be able to not do their job, receive a pension and ride off into the sunset" (Miller & Madan, 2018). Philip Schentrup (the father of Carmen Schentrup) also argued that Peterson "heard the gunfire, and he knew what it was … His training wasn't to clear the area, it was to immediately engage the shooter and stop the killing. He must live with himself and the truth that 17 people were murdered as he stood around and did nothing" (Miller & Madan, 2018). These statements all function to increase the offensiveness of Peterson's activities during the shooting by emphasizing that he had a special responsibility as a police officer to protect the children from harm.

## Peterson's Inaction Caused Innocent Victims to be Killed

Other attacks sought to increase offensiveness by emphasizing that the victims of the horrific shooting were innocent or helpless. Scott Israel stated in his press conference: "Devastated. Sick to my stomach. There are no words. These families lost their children. We lost coaches. I've been the funerals. I've been to the homes where they sit and shiver. I've been to the vigils. It's just … uh … there are no words" (Sun Sentinel, 2018). Later in his interview on *CNN*, he would articulate a similar position: "If Scot Peterson went into … do I believe if Scot Peterson went into … into that building there was a chance he could have neutralized the killer and saved lives, yes I believe that. But as far as anything else done at this point, I can't say that" (CNN, 2018). Although he didn't explicitly say the victims were innocent or helpless, he made it clear that Peterson's intervention would have helped prevent the loss of innocent lives. The parents of the victims also expressed their frustration at the unnecessary loss of defenseless children. For example, Fred Guttenberg said, "He is responsible in large part for my why my daughter is gone and I have no sympathy for him, I'm glad he's been arrested" (Miller & Madan, 2018). April Schentrup also expressed, "I can just say that my kid is no longer here. We understand human errors, but we don't understand why our children are no longer here when other things could have been done, could've helped prevent this" (Miller & Madan, 2018). These statements from Guttenberg and Schentrup make it clear that the victims were children and that they have to live out the remainder of their lives without them.

## Peterson was a Coward and Unmotivated to Act

Other attacks focused on Peterson's character. These attacks functioned to enhance the perception that the target possessed a certain trait. Many of them used the strategy of arguing that the accused had performed acts consistent with a certain trait. For example, Scott Israel argued during an interview with CBS Miami: "Peterson didn't go in because he was afraid. No other reason" (CBS Miami, 2019). Although brief, the statement attached the trait of cowardice to Peterson and then made clear that the evidence of that cowardice was Peterson's decision not to engage with the shooter. Then President Donald Trump also accused Peterson of being a coward: "When it came time to get in there and do something, he didn't have the courage or something happened" (Lima, 2018). This statement also attaches the trait of cowardice to Peterson and argues his decision to remain stationary during the crisis was a direct result of his lack of courage. Trump also argued that Peterson had an attitude of indifference toward the students: "I'd rather have somebody who loves their students and wants to protect their students than someone standing outside who doesn't know anybody." This statement implies that Peterson's failure to act was a direct result of the character trait of indifference or not being emotionally invested in the students he was charged with protecting.

## Peterson Attempted to Portray Himself as a Victim

Other attacks would argue that Peterson was making statements consistent with a particular trait. For example, Fred Guttenberg said, "I'm tired of him trying to paint himself as the victim. He is not a victim. He created victims. He keeps referring to them as his kids. They are not your kids, Scot Peterson! You let them die!" (Miller & Madan, 2018). Similarly, another parent, Philip Schentrup, argued, "He is attempting to create a narrative about him as a victim instead of the truth" (Miller & Madan, 2018). Both of these statements function to enhance the audience's perception that Peterson possesses a particular negative trait. The parents argue that Peterson's effort to move attention away from the 17 victims of the shooting to himself and the discomfort that resulted from public scrutiny about his negligence demonstrates his lack of humanity or compassion for the suffering of others.

# Observations and Conclusions

The persuasive attack on Scot Peterson for his failure to act on behalf of the Marjory Stoneman Douglas students seemed to be effective. Formal charges were eventually brought against Peterson for child neglect, but legal experts believed those charges would be difficult to prove because the law had only historically been applied to caregivers (Simon, 2019). The decision to prosecute in spite of the legal hurdles may be evidence that the tide of negative public sentiment toward Peterson was too great to ignore. Also, it may not be a coincidence that the key attack (the obligation to protect the victims) aligned perfectly with the legal argument that Peterson was, in fact, a special caregiver to these students. Most people facing momentary life-and-death decisions are not accountable for their fear or failure to act. However, Peterson's police training was supposed to take away the "uncertainty" of the moment and compel him to not only act but to act quickly. He did not. The attacks against Peterson functioned especially well to keep his sworn oath of duty as the salient issue for the public. Thus, this case demonstrates that an individual's role in society may open them up for greater attack, thereby limiting their rhetorical options for a response.

The strategy of increasing offensiveness by emphasizing that the victims were innocent was likely to be compelling to audiences, as it is clearly much worse to not intervene during a shooting where children are involved. The parents' emotionally charged statements were likely to resonate with other parents, who could imagine the anger they too would feel if their child could have been saved by the hands of a braver officer. If the person hiding behind the building had been a regular staff member and not law enforcement, the parents would likely have been disappointed but compassionate and understanding.

Sheriff Scott Israel's attacks were temporarily effective in displacing responsibility for his poor leadership and keeping the focus squarely on Peterson. It wasn't until the following year that Florida Governor Ron DeSantis would also hold Israel responsible and suspend him for "incompetence and dereliction of duty for actions before and after the mass shooting at Marjory Stoneman Douglas High School in Parkland" (Allen, 2019). Israel denied any personal failure of leadership and vowed to run again at the soonest opportunity.

The character attacks on Peterson were equally effective. They argued that he was a coward, emotionally distant from those he was charged with protecting, and that he shamelessly tried to portray himself as a victim when the victims were clearly the deceased. Obviously, people make mistakes, and those mistakes often have severe consequences. In this case, combining the strategies of increasing the level of responsibility, the level of offensiveness, and the fact that significant character flaws led to the behavior had a cumulative effect on portraying Peterson as an uncaring, cowardly man who turned his back on his sworn oath to protect and then made the situation worse by seeking to generate sympathy for himself.

This case reveals that in some apologetic situations, public sentiment is elevated when the people involved have a special obligation to protect those under their charge. The prosecutors were compelled to move quickly with the prosecution due to the wave of parental and media scrutiny. It is worth noting that the attacks were coming from multiple directions and seemingly all levels of the public sphere, reaching as high as former President Donald Trump calling Petersen a "coward."

Petersen was considered more culpable for this offense, even though he was not the perpetrator who carried out this heinous act; rather, he was a trained resource officer, wherein the public assumption is that his training should override any level of uncertainty. Thus, the strategy of increasing negative perceptions of the act by demonstrating Petersen's obligation to protect his victims because they are innocent and helpless is an effective tool for weakening any subsequent explanation Petersen could offer.

Sheriff Scott Israel attacked Petersen directly and allowed others to attack him to avoid criticism himself. His decision demonstrates the impact that the strategies of enhancing perceptions that the target possesses a trait and acts consistent with the trait have are effective. The character attacks were more impactful in this case because he demonstrated cowardice not only behaviorally but also rhetorically as he tried to portray himself as the real victim in a situation where he should have been the hero.

# References

Allen, G. (2019, October 21). Committee backs suspension of Broward sheriff over 2018 school shooting. *NPR.* https://www.npr.org/2019/10/21/772140046/committee-backs-suspension-of-broward-sheriff-over-2018-high-school-shootings

Bacon, J. (2018, June 7). Parkland parents enraged by 'coward' deputy Scot Peterson's explanation for not entering school. *USA Today.* https://www.usatoday.com/story/news/nat

ion/2018/06/07/florida-school-shooting-scot-petersons-explanation-outrages-parents/681182002/

Broward Sheriff Scott Israel reveals school resource officer never went in during Parkland Shooting. (2018, March 1). *YouTube*. https://www.youtube.com/watch?v=8PvXJxBXW88

CBS Miami. (2019, November 1). *Former BSO officer Scott Israel responds to senate removal, criticisms of performance* [Video]. YouTube. https://www.youtube.com/watch?v=KWa9Y8qxoCY

Chavez, N. (2018a, March 8). What happened, moment by moment, in the Florida school massacre. *CNN*. https://www.cnn.com/2018/02/15/us/florida-school-shooting-timeline/index.html

Chavez, N. (2018b, June 4). This is what Scot Peterson did during the Parkland school shooting. *CNN*. https://www.cnn.com/2019/06/04/us/parkland-scot-peterson-actions/index.html

Chuck, E., Johnson, A., & Siemaszko, C. (2018, February 15). 17 killed in mass shooting at high school in Parkland, Florida. *NBC News*. https://www.nbcnews.com/news/us-news/police-respond-shooting-parkland-florida-high-school-n848101

CNN. (2018, February 25). *Tapper grills Sheriff Israel over school shooting response* [Video]. YouTube. https://www.youtube.com/watch?v=GfGJ_SRcBSE&t=2s

Dusenbury, W. (2018, February 22). Aaron Geis, beloved football coach died saving students, mourned by Stoneman Douglas community. *South Florida Sun Sentinel*. https://www.sun-sentinel.com/local/broward/parkland/florida-school-shooting/fl-florida-school-shooting-aaron-feis-funeral-20180222-story.html

Hassan, A. (2019, June 6). Scot Peterson is released on bond. Here's how he's explained his actions during the Parkland Shooting. *New York Times*. https://www.nytimes.com/2019/06/06/us/scot-peterson-parkland-shooting.html

Lima, C. (2018, February 23). Trump: Florida deputy who sought cover during shooting 'doesn't love the children'. *Politico*. https://www.politico.com/story/2018/02/23/trump-florida-deputy-scot-peterson-422742

Miller, C. M., & Madan, M. O. (2018, June 4). "It's all crap:" Parents lash out in anger after Parkland cop Scot Peterson ends silence. *Miami Herald*. https://www.miamiherald.com/news/local/community/broward/article212483719.html

Simon, D. (2019, June 8). Why the case against former Marjory Stoneman Douglas resource officer Scot Peterson is the first of its kind. *CNN*. https://www.cnn.com/2019/06/08/us/parkland-scot-peterson-child-neglect-charges/index.html

Stracqualursi, V. (2018, February 23). Trump: Parkland deputy 'didn't have the courage'. *CNN*. https://www.cnn.com/2018/02/23/politics/trump-deputy-sheriff-florida-shooting/index.html

Sun Sentinel (2018, March 1). *Broward Sheriff Scott Israel reveals school resource officer never went in during Parkland shooting* [Video]. YouTube. https://www.youtube.com/watch?v=8PvXJxBXW88

Susskind, S., & Rodriguez, J. (2019, June 4). Former Broward County deputy Scot Peterson appears in court following arrrest. *WPTV West Palm Beach*. https://www.wptv.com/news/parkland-shooting/former-deputy-scot-peterson-arrested-for-child-neglect-following-parkland-school-shooting

# · 11 ·

## *THE MAIDEN TRIBUTE OF MODERN BABYLON*: CHILD SEX TRAFFICKING IN VICTORIAN LONDON

Victorian England is often thought of as a strait-laced society that embraced a puritan morality. In a shocking incident in 1885, William T. Stead published an expose of child prostitution in London, *The Maiden Tribute of Modern Babylon* (2011). Stead was a prominent journalist, editor, and social advocate at the time, covering not only child prostitution but also universal education, votes for women, the repeal of the Contagious Acts, and the Irish Home Rule. He was also a stronger supporter of the Salvation Army and the Liberal Party (Spartacus-Educational, n.d.; Whyte, 1925). In one of his more renowned investigations, Stead's persuasive attack on child prostitution in Victorian England was serialized in *The Pall Mall Gazette* during July of 1885. Stead seized on the Greek myth of the Minotaur (Garcia, 2013) to encapsulate his accusations. He reminded readers that in this myth, the city of Athens sent a tribute of young men and women to Crete to satiate the hunger of this terrible monster. To placate the fearsome Minotaur, Athens was forced "to send once every nine years a tribute to Crete of seven youths and seven maidens." These victims were thrown "into the famous Labyrinth of Daedalus, there to wander about blindly until such time as they were devoured by the Minotaur, a frightful monster" (Stead, 2011, p.7). He draws an explicit comparison between the Minotaur and London by declaring that "This very night in London, and every night, year in and year out, not seven maidens but many times seven ... will be offered up as the Maiden Tribute of Modern Babylon" (p.8). Babylon "owes its fame (or infamy) to the many references the Bible makes to it; all of which are unfavorable" (Ancient History Encyclopedia, 2021). To label London in 1885 a "modern Babylon" was a serious accusation.

This chapter reports an analysis of the strategies of persuasive attack in *The Maiden Tribute of Modern Babylon*. This discourse focuses on offensive acts committed in Victorian London. Although the actions alleged here had implications for the character of the perpetrators, the text and this analysis focus on acts rather than character. As such, this text will be analyzed for the use of strategies for increasing negative perceptions of the acts and increasing perceived responsibility for these actions, as discussed in the book's introductory chapter. Three accusations will be addressed in this chapter: children were sold, children were bought, and children were violated. Although these offensive acts are clearly interrelated (and share common victims), this analysis will address these accusations separately.

## Strategies of Persuasive Attack in The Maiden Tribute of Modern Babylon

This text advances three interrelated reprehensible attacks: (1) that children are sold into prostitution; (2) that children are purchased for prostitution; and (3) that children are sexually violated. These accusations should be discussed separately because each of these offenses has a different offender or perpetrator: parents (and others) sell the victims, brothel-keepers (or others) buy the victims, and yet a third group of villains violate the victims. Selling or buying humans, although offensive in and of itself, does not necessarily involve sexual assault. So, these three ideas should be considered three separate accusations.

## The Sale of Children

The accusation that children were sold in Victorian London addressed both of the basic elements of a persuasive attack: the offensiveness of the act and responsibility for the act. Each of these two aspects will be addressed next.

## Increasing Negative Perceptions of the Act

One method of increasing the perceived offensiveness of an act is to argue that it occurs repeatedly: "Drunken parents often sell their children to brothel-keepers" (p.19). This statement indicates that this act is not rare but occurs often. This message hints at another strategy: that the offenders (mothers) had an obligation to protect the victim, but the text does not explicitly make this argument. A London brothel-keeper explained, "Many women who are on the streets have female children. They are worth keeping. When they get to be twelve or thirteen they become merchantable" (p.19). The idea of selling another human being is clearly repugnant on its face, thereby making these types of attacks more impactful.

## Increasing Perceived Responsibility for the Act

Stead also addressed the question of responsibility for these offensive acts, indicating that the mothers benefitted from selling their children. For example, the attack explained that the victims' "mothers sometimes consent to their seduction for the sake of the price paid by their seducer" (p. 30). One mother overheard negotiations for the sale of a virgin between 13 and 14 years old. She then "whispered eagerly to the seller, 'Don't you think she would take our Lily?'" Stead revealed that "Lily was her own daughter, a bright, fresh-looking little girl, who was thirteen years old" (p.32). Stead gave an example to illustrate this point: "My old friend … agreed to hand over her own child, a pretty girl of eleven, for £5" (p.21). Those who sold children were directly responsible for these reprehensible acts, having benefited from them.

## The Purchase of Children

The second accusation in this attack is that children were purchased. Obviously, this observation follows from the first, yet buyer and seller are different parties to the offensive act. Again, both offensiveness and blame are addressed in *The Maiden Tribute of Modern Babylon*. These elements will be discussed in this section.

## Increasing Negative Perceptions of the Act

As shown in the second attack, many children had been sold in London (the extent of the harm). Furthermore, those in this loathsome trade confirmed that children were bought. One brothel-keeper said, "The getting of fresh girls takes time, but it is simple and easy enough" (p.19). Stead also reported that these victims "are regularly procured, bought at so much per head" (p.15). One landlady admitted that she had repeatedly bought and sold children: "I remember selling two maids for £20 each, one at £16, one at £15, one at £13 and others for less. Of course where I bought I paid less than that" (p.24). Clearly, the purchase of children in London was an offensive act that occurred over and over.

## Increasing Responsibility for the Act

Stead indicated that brothel-keepers actively planned the acquisition of girls for violation, for these victims were "recruited for as diligently as is the army of her Majesty" (p.41). He observed that "the recruiting for brothels is … a systematized business" (p.51). Furthermore, he explained that "Every brothel-keeper worth her salt is a procuress with her eyes constantly on the lookout for likely girls, and she is quite as busy weaving toils in which to ensnare fresh women as she is to command fresh customers" (p.41). Without question, these offenders planned these offensive acts, which solidifies their undeniable responsibility.

# The Violation of Children

The final attack focuses on the violations committed by these children. As horrible as the buying and selling of children is by itself, the sexual abuse of these girls is even worse. Stead discusses the offensiveness of, and the blame for, these reprehensible acts.

## Increasing Negative Perceptions of Act

Stead's attack addressed the effects on the victims. He laments that these victims "have lost what woman ought to value more than life" (p. 15). These violations of children are characterized as a "crime of the most ruthless and abominable description" (p. 11). In one case, the perpetrator took a young woman, "drugged her, seduced her, and communicated to her a foul and loathsome disease" (p. 89). A woman who managed a brothel explained that girls were,

> drugged ... a mixture of laudanum and something else. Sometimes chloroform is used ... We call it drowse or black draught and they lie almost as if dead, and the girl never knows what has happened till morning. And then? Oh! Then she cries a great deal from the pain, but she is mazed and hardly knows what has happened except that she can hardly move from pain. (p.24)

Furthermore, victims who were not violated while unconscious suffered during, as well as after, their violation. One vile woman stated, "that whenever the girl was fourteen or fifteen years of age she should be strapped down hand and foot to the four posts of the bedstead, so that all resistance save that of unavailing screaming would be impossible" (p. 31). Other victims died from their violation: Stead reported, "Most of those ensnared tonight will perish, some of them in horrible torture" (p.9). The suffering these victims were forced to endure is monstrous.

*The Maiden Tribute of Modern Babylon* also stressed the extent of these abominable acts. Stead emphasizes the distressing frequency of these violations: "Multitudes are swept irresistibly on and on to be destroyed in due season, to give place to others, who will also share their doom. The maw of the London Minotaur is insatiable" (p.9). The attack reported that, "These outrages are constantly perpetrated" (p.14). In fact, a single person bragged that "he has ruined 3,000 women in his time" (p.94). One brothel-keeper confirmed that she had supplied "one gentleman with seventy fresh maids every year" (p.57). These statements leave no doubt that many, many children were violated in London.

This attack also lamented the fact that these victims were innocent or helpless: "Children of twelve and thirteen cannot offer any serious resistance" to their violation (p.30). Stead also observed, "The victims of the rapes, for all intents and purposes, are almost always very young children between thirteen and fifteen" (p.39). Two procurers of flesh explained that, "their real work, to which they devote every day in the week, is the purveying of maidens to an extensive and ever-widening circle of customers" (p.52). Stead explained, "These virgins are mostly of a tender age, being too young in fact to understand the nature of the crime of which they are the unwilling victims" (p.14). At the time, the age of consent in England was 13 years, so although all of these sexual attacks were morally wrong and deeply offensive, not all were actually criminal acts.

## Increasing Perceived Responsibility for the Act

Stead argued that these cruel violations were planned. He explained that child violation "is constantly and systematically practiced in London without let or hindrance" (p.11). Similarly, he averred that, "there is in full operation among us a system in which the violation of virgins is one of the ordinary incidents" (p.14). Further evidence of planning came from his description of the rooms prepared for these loathsome acts. "Some of the houses had an underground room from which no sound could be heard ... Padded rooms for the purpose of stifling the cries of tortured victims of lust and brutality" (p.28). Stead gave an example of one of these chambers:

> Here is a room where you can be perfectly secure. The house sounds on its own grounds. The walls are thick, there is a double carpet on the floor. The only window which fronts upon the back garden is doubly secured, first with shutters and then with heavy curtain. You lock the door and then you can do as you please. The girl may scream blue murder but not a sound will be heard. (p.29)

In fact, Stead concluded, "the arrangements for procuring, certifying, violating, repairing, and disposing of these ruined victims of the lust of London are made with a simplicity and efficiency incredible to all" (pp. 14–15). There can be no doubt that these perpetrators carefully planned these heinous violations.

# Observations and Conclusions

This persuasive attack convincingly addresses both the offensiveness (repeated offense, extent of harm, effects on victims, innocent victims) and the blame (accused benefit, planned offense) for this offensive behavior. As such, it clearly illustrates the strategies of the Theory of Persuasive Attack. One result of this persuasive attack was that Stead was imprisoned for three months because he had conducted an illegal investigation, but this work also prompted the enactment of the Criminal Law Amendment Act of 1885, raising the age of consent from 13 years old to 16 years old in this country ("The Maiden Tribute," 2021).

In this case, the combined impact of planning the offense and helpless or innocent victims is likely the strongest strategy. Truly, only purely evil people would orchestrate something so harmful to children in the name of financial and immoral gain. In addition, Stead's attack also reveals that repeated behaviors are more offensive than isolated cases, because isolated cases can be excused based on unique circumstances or by feigning ignorance.

One interesting insight is that one attack can have a ripple effect. For instance, the traffickers themselves would be the primary target of the attack, but the impact of that attack easily bleeds over to other culpable parties. The attacks were especially damaging to the mothers involved, who were accused of benefiting from selling their children. The reason this argument is especially effective is that the audience would likely believe that the most important thing to any mother would be her children and not money or notoriety. While we have argued that the idea of selling another human being is repugnant, the act becomes even more heinous when it comes from another person charged with protecting the victim.

This case also establishes that an effective method for elevating an attack is to argue that the effects will persist for the duration of the victims' lives. In this case, the girls who were violated will inevitably face emotional trauma for decades following such reprehensible crimes. Clearly, most attacks will make use of multiple strategies for increasing responsibility and offensiveness.

# References

Ancient History Encyclopedia. (2021). Babylon. https://www.ancient.eu/babylon/

Garcia, B. (2013, September 1). Minotaur. *World History Encyclopedia*. https://www.worldhistory.org/Minotaur/

Spartacus-Educational (n.d.). William Stead. https://spartacus-educational.com/Jstead.htm

Stead, W. T. (1885; reprinted 2011). *The maiden tribute of modern Babylon: The report of our secret commission*. Pall Mall Gazette, July 1885. Lowood Press (CreateSpace).

The Maiden Tribute of Modern Babylon. (2021). *Wikipedia*. https://en.wikipedia.org/wiki/The_Maiden_Tribute_of_Modern_Babylon

Whyte, F. (1925). *The life of W. T. Stead*, Volume 1. J. Cape Limited.

# BLACKFISH: TILIKUM WAS LITERALLY A KILLER WHALE

SeaWorld is a chain of aquatic theme parks that was started in San Diego in 1964 and features orcas (killer whales), sea lions, and dolphins. It expanded over time, and in 2021, it operated aquatic parks in multiple locations.

Florida: SeaWorld Orlando, Discovery Cove Orlando, AquaticaOrlando, Busch Gardens Tampa Bay, Adventure Island Tampa
California: SeaWorld San Diego and Aquatica San Diego
Texas: SeaWorld San Antonio, Aquatica San Antonio, and Discovery Point
Virginia: Busch Gardens Williamsburg and Water Country USA
Pennsylvania: Sesame Place

SeaWorld Orlando is a popular tourist destination. For example, in 2009, before the *Blackfish* controversy discussed here, almost six million people visited this particular aquatic theme park ("Attendance at the SeaWorld Florida," 2021). However, a serious and potentially devastating controversy arose the next year, which threatened the viability of this enterprise.

In February of 2010, the orca Tilikum killed a trained and experienced female diver, Dawn Brancheau. Sadly, this was not an isolated incident, as Tilikum had been involved in the deaths of other people in the past. In response to this controversy, *Blackfish* (2013), a documentary film attacking

SeaWorld over Tilikum, offered a scathing criticism of Seaworld's operation, where highly intelligent and responsive animals are kept in captivity (IMDB, n.d.). CNN reports that when *Blackfish* was broadcast on this network, "nearly 21 million people watched" (Kuo & Savidge, 2014). After this documentary, many bands or artists pulled out of events scheduled at SeaWorld parks in protest, including Martina McBride, 38 Special, REO Speedwagon, Cheap Trick, Heart, Barenaked Ladies, Trisha Yearwood, and Willie Nelson (Duke, 2013). Attendance at the San Diego SeaWorld "plunged 17%" in 2014 (Van Grove, 2015), and SeaWorld's profits fell by 84% in the second quarter alone in 2015 (Rhodan, 2015). In the same year, Southwest Airlines announced that it would not renew its partnership with SeaWorld. The fallout from this documentary was substantial.

Welsh (2015) concluded, "The publicity disaster that followed the movie's release in 2013 was likely the turning point for SeaWorld. The company announced Monday, November 9, that it will phase out killer whale shows in their San Diego amusement park by 2017" (para. 3). Attorneys for the Occupational Safety and Health Administration (OSHA) indicated that "SeaWorld only made changes after trainer Dawn Brancheau's death outraged the public" (CNN Transcripts, 2013). This case study extends previous work on the rhetoric of documentary film (Benson & Snee, 2008; Blakesley, 2003; Medhurst & Benson, 1984) by examining the persuasive attacks in the *Blackfish* documentary.

## Persuasive Attack on *Blackfish*

This message employs: (1) strategies for intensifying the offensiveness of the act; and (2) strategies for enhancing responsibility for that action. These two elements of a persuasive attack on SeaWorld's actions will be discussed separately in this chapter. Please note that all quotations in this section are from *Blackfish*.

## Intensifying Offensiveness

*Blackfish* worked to increase the offensiveness of SeaWorld's use of killer whales in its shows in two ways. First, it argued that the orca attacks on its victims were terrible acts (although not explored in this chapter, the documentary argues that orcas generally and Tilikum in particular had been maltreated). Second, the documentary sought to enhance sympathy for the victims.

## Extent and Persistence of Effects

The strategy of "extensiveness" typically refers to the frequency with which the offensive act occurs. However, an action can be shown to be serious by describing the effects in horrific details. The documentary began with a recording of a 911 call: "We need a response for a dead person at Sea World. A whale has eaten one of the trainers." The film reported that Dawn "was scalped, and there was no blood, so pretty much we knew then that the heart wasn't beating." As terrible as this was, it got even worse as Detective Revere from the Orange County Sheriff's Office interviewed Seaworld Paramedic Thomas Tobin:

> Revere: Once they were able to pull her away, how did he let go of the arm?
> Tobin: He didn't.
> Revere: He never let go of the arm?
> Tobin: He swallowed it.

Dawn Brancheau was savagely killed by Tilikum. This killer whale bit off her scalp and her arm and then swallowed her arm. She suffered "evulsion [forcible extraction of a body part], laceration, abrasion, fractures. Fractures and associated hemorrhages, blunt force traumas to the main body, to the extremities." The film explained that "these were vicious killer whales that had 48 sharp teeth that would rip you to shreds if they got a chance." The documentary showed a video clip of a killer whale swimming up underneath a trainer and pushing her high in the air. This "trick" was shown again, stressing how much larger and more powerful orcas were than trainers.

Dawn Brancheau was not the first trainer killed by this whale. Before he was bought by SeaWorld, Tilikum was part of the show at Sealand in Canada. In 1991, Keltie Byrne, a 21-year-old, was killed by Tilikum and two other whales. The documentary relied on eyewitnesses to report Keltie's death:

> Her foot just dipped into the edge of the pool and she lost her balance and fell in ... the whale zoomed over, grabbed her boot, and pulled her back in ... She started to scream ... And then they would pull her under, and then they would come up ... And then they'd take her down again ... So it was harder and harder for her to get that air in because she was screaming. And my sister remembers her saying "I don't

want to die!" We couldn't help her. It was really wretched ... She was pulled under by the whale.

Keltie Byrne was another excruciating and tragic death involving Tilikum, leading Sealand to close and SeaWorld to purchase Tilikum.

In 1999, also before Brancheau's death, Daniel Dukes (not a trainer) was found dead in a whale tank at SeaWorld. The film reported the revolting account of Dukes' death: "Tilikum stripped him, bit off his genitals, [and] there were bite marks all over his body." Dukes was found "draped over the back of Tilikum." The film said in the morning, "there was Tilikum with a dead, naked guy on his back, kind of parading him around the back pool." This was another instance of orcas behaving literally as killer whales, viciously attacking and killing humans.

Other debilitating accidents occurred that did not result in death, yet there were still serious attacks. In 1987, John Sillick "was crushed between two whales at SeaWorld of San Diego." *Blackfish* included video showing Sillick riding one whale when another whale jumped up and landed on him. He was seriously injured, as the film relates: "What kept his body together was that his wetsuit basically held him together. I know he's had multiple surgeries and he's got tons of hardware in his body." In 2002, two other SeaWorld orcas grabbed trainer Tamari Tollison by her foot: "She's under the water, Splash and Orkid both have her ...You hear her just scream out 'somebody help me!' And the way she screamed it was just bloodcurdling; she knew she was going to die. Her arm, it was U-shaped. It was compound-fractured. She's very lucky to be alive, that's for sure." Four years later in 2006, the orca Kasatka grabbed trainer Ken Peters' foot

> and dragged him to the bottom of the pool and held him at the bottom ... let him go, picked him up, took him down again ... Ken Peters pulled himself over the float line and swam ... to a slide-out ... The whale jumped over and went right after him. He tried to stand up and run but of course his feet were damaged, he just fell and scrambled ... [It was] a hair's breadth away from another fatality.

*Blackfish* showed the video as yet another instance of a vicious attack on a trainer by a SeaWorld orca.

## Sympathy for Victim

Such deaths would be tragic, no matter who had been killed. However, the documentary intensified the offensiveness of this particular death: "She's beautiful, she's blonde, she's athletic, she's friendly, everybody loves Dawn [Brancheau]." Her sister stated, "Dawn was the most loving, giving person you ever met. Her smile just radiated." The film played clips of Brancheau being interviewed, portraying her as a lovely, friendly young woman. These clips were interlaced with videos of Brancheau swimming with orcas and being pushed up in the air. Keltie Byrne, another victim, was characterized as a "championship swimmer." Video clips showed her swimming and giving an interview in which she said her goal was "to swim fast at nationals." These positive depictions of the victims intensified the offensiveness of their deaths.

## The Offensive Acts Were Repeated

Earlier, as we established that the use of killer whales was dangerous, we recounted repeated deaths: Dawn Brancheau, Keltie Byrne, and Daniel Dukes. The film observed that, "what happened to her [Brancheau] really could have happened to anyone." Furthermore, other trainers were attacked and severely injured by killer whales: John Sillick, Tamari Tollison, and Ken Peters. In total, *Blackfish* reported that, "it's 70+, maybe even more, just killer whale/trainer accidents." The film displayed pages from a report about orca/trainer incidents to reinforce this idea. Notice that this repetition of offensive acts (orca attacks) reinforces the offensiveness discussed earlier. It is important to realize that the offensive acts committed by SeaWorld were not the deaths themselves, although it was responsible for them. The real calamity was SeaWorld's decision to continue to use dangerous killer whales in shows for years.

These elements of persuasive attack worked well together to establish the offensiveness of SeaWorld's use of killer whales in their shows. These deaths were truly horrific, and the victims clearly deserve our sympathy.

# Enhancing Responsibility

*Blackfish* enhanced the responsibility of SeaWorld through three strategies: (1) it knew the potential consequences of using killer whales in its shows; (2) it benefited from using these orcas; and (3) it repeated the offense. Each idea will be discussed in this section.

## SeaWorld Knew the Consequences

Killer whales could be very dangerous. OSHA sued SeaWorld, arguing that "swimming with orcas is inherently dangerous and that you can't completely predict the outcome when you enter the water or enter their environment." A commercial promoting SeaWorld featured actor James Earl Jones explaining that a killer whale weighs 8,000 pounds. A former trainer commented, "It's shocking to see how large they are." SeaWorld can hardly claim killer whales are not dangerous, as even its own advertising campaign acknowledges the size of these animals.

The documentary developed the idea that SeaWorld was aware that Tilikum, in particular, was dangerous. The day he arrived at SeaWorld, a trainer approached the killer whale: "One of the supervisors said 'get her outta there!' And just screamed at her, 'get her away from there'....I remember thinking why are you guys making such a big deal out of this?" Clearly, management thought there was some reason to exercise caution around him. This event shows that SeaWorld was aware of the potential danger Tilikum posed.

Furthermore, a 911 call made the day of Brancheau's death was reported, "We actually have a trainer in the water with one of our whales, the whale that they're not supposed to be in the water with." Why would someone from SeaWorld say a trainer was "not supposed to be in the water with" Tilikum? This admission indicates that the company knew this orca was dangerous. The film also reported the argument that "It's pretty outrageous that SeaWorld would claim there was no expecting Tilikum to come out of the water because they had witnessed him coming out of the water and it's written into his profile; He lunges at trainers." The video displayed this SeaWorld training document and then highlighted the idea that Tilikum was capable of "sometimes lunging toward a control trainer." These statements demonstrate that SeaWorld knew that Tilikum was a deadly threat.

## The Accused Benefited

Shows featuring killer whales were very popular, as suggested earlier. This spectacle means that "The industry has a vested interest in spinning these [performances] so that the animals continue to appear like cuddly teddy bears that are completely safe. You know, that sells a lot of Shamu dolls. It sells a lot of tickets at the gate." It turns out that Tilikum was a valuable corporate asset.

Furthermore, the company bought and used Tilikum as a source of sperm for breeding: "When SeaWorld heard that Tilikum was available after this accident at Sealand, they really wanted Tilikum because they needed a breeder." Greed overruled caution when SeaWorld bought Tillikum. It appears that orca sperm can generate substantial income for SeaWorld. The film mused: "This guy [Tilikum was a male orca], his proven track record of killing people, he's clearly a liability to the institution. Why keep him around? Well, it's quite simple … his semen is worth a lot of money …" Over the years, Tilikum has been one of the main breeding whales at SeaWorld. However, SeaWorld kept Tillikum because he was a commodity that provided a financial benefit to the company. The threat represented by Tilikum could well be promulgated through his DNA: "In the entire SeaWorld collection, it's like 54% of the whales on SeaWorld's collection now have Tilikum's genes." This greed could wreak havoc on future generations.

Two strategies of persuasive attack worked together here to establish blame: (1) SeaWorld knew Tilikum was dangerous yet continued to use him in shows; and (2) SeaWorld benefitted from keeping Tilikum. Definitively, *Blackfish* established that this company was responsible for these deaths.

## Observations and Conclusions

This analysis underscores the point that documentaries, particularly those that show unfiltered and sometimes graphic video clips, can be used effectively in persuasive attack. Video contributed to both key elements of a persuasive attacks, increasing offensiveness and enhancing responsibility for an offense. In the introduction to this chapter, we showed that *Blackfish* had instigated a backlash against SeaWorld and forced it to end shows involving killer whales. Those who care about both animals and humans can be grateful for *Blackfish* for exposing this offensive action, establishing blame, and getting this problem corrected. Both elements of persuasive attack were employed in this example of public advocacy. The offensiveness of the act was developed by arguing the extent of the harms, by invoking sympathy for victims, and by arguing that the harms were repeated. Responsibility for the act was shown by indicating that SeaWorld was aware of the consequences of their actions and that they benefited from the act. Perpetrating unspeakable harm, doing so repeatedly, and knowing the consequences of the behavior in advance provide a strong combination of attack strategies because together they preempt some of the more likely responses in defense of the behavior (e.g., the incident was not that bad, it only happened one time, or I was unaware of what was happening). Previous literature on attack has virtually ignored documentary film as an important medium for attack as well as the mileage that can be gained by focusing on the victims of attack and the trauma they experience from a person or organization's harmful behavior.

One indirect consideration is that behavioral attacks inadvertently create an artificial binary about the character of people who may reside on the periphery of the attack itself. For instance, it is one thing to say that Seaworld and their leadership placed humans and animals in danger, but it is another to ask the question about why. Thus, the audience is left with the realization that corporate leaders are entirely motivated by profit, or worse, they are evil people who hold no regard for employee and animal safety. When behavioral attacks are done well, the audience will make their own judgments about character without those statements ever being expressed.

# References

Attendance at the Seaworld Florida theme park from 2009 to 2019 (in millions). (2020). *Statista.* https://www.statista.com/statistics/236187/attendance-at-the-seaworld-florida-theme-park

Benson, T. W., & Snee, B. J. (Eds.). (2008). *The rhetoric of the new political documentary.* Southern Illinois University Press.

*Blackfish.* (2013). Magnolia Pictures and CNN Films.

Blakesley, D. (2003). *The terministic screen: Rhetorical perspectives on film.* Southern Illinois University Press.

CNN Transcripts (2013, October 24). Blackfish: The truth behind keeping marine animals captive. https://transcripts.cnn.com/show/se/date/2013-10-24/segment/02

Duke, A. (2013, December 16). Martina McBride, 38 Special, cancel SeaWorld gig over 'Blackfish' backlash. *CNN.* https://www.cnn.com/2013/12/16/showbiz/seaworld-martina-mcbride-cancels/index.html

IMDB (n.d.). *Blackfish.* https://www.imdb.com/title/tt2545118/?ref_=fn_al_tt_1

Kuo, V., & Savidge, M. (2014, February 9). Months after "Blackfish" airs, debate over orcas continues. *CNN.* https://www.cnn.com/2014/02/07/us/blackfish-wrap

Medhurst, M. J., & Benson, T. W. (1984). *Rhetorical dimensions in media: A critical casebook.* Kendall Hunt.

Rhodan, M. (2015, August 6). Seaworld's profits drop 84% after *Blackfish* documentary. *TIME.* https://time.com/3987998/seaworlds-profits-drop-84-after-blackfish-documentary/

Van Grove, J. (2015, November 9). SeaWorld to end theatrical killer whale show. *San Diego Union-Tribune.* https://www.sandiegouniontribune.com/business/tourism/sdut-seaworld-san-diego-phase-out-killer-whale-show-2015nov09-story.html

Welsh, J. (2015, November 9). This chilling movie is probably behind SeaWorld's decision to close a killer whale exhibit. *Business Insider.* https://www.businessinsider.com/blackfish-movie-seaworld-san-diego-2015-11

# Part V
## PERSUASIVE ATTACK IN OTHER CONTEXTS

Persuasive attack is part and parcel of human endeavor. To further investigate the scope of this phenomenon, this chapter takes a different approach from others in this book. Rather than choosing a single text (or related group of texts, such as Republican selfies), this chapter offers brief illustrations from a variety of contexts: a viral YouTube video, poetry by John Lithgow, late-night television, tabloid newspapers, a stump speech from a former president, commercial comparative advertising, seventeenth-century English ballads, and the American colonies. This chapter provides support for the claim that persuasive attack pervades society in a wide variety of media.

## "United Breaks Guitars": Persuasive Attack via YouTube

United Airlines is one of the largest carriers in the airline industry. In 2008, United flew 66 million passengers generating revenues of $15.24 billion ("United Airlines Statistics," 2021). This company is worthy of scholarly attention. One group of passengers who flew United on March 31, 2008, was musician Dave Carroll and his band, Sons of Maxwell. While they were waiting on the tarmac at Chicago O'Hare Airport, another passenger on the plane exclaimed that the baggage crew was throwing guitars around outside the plane. Carroll realized this horseplay probably involved his guitar and tried to alert members of the flight crew on his airplane. Unfortunately, they ignored his pleas for help. When they arrived at their destination, Carroll's prized Taylor guitar (worth $3500) was damaged and could not be played. Carroll filed claims for damage; United made several excuses (e.g., it claimed he signed a damage waiver; it claimed he filed his claim too late) but repeatedly refused to provide him any help (Carroll, 2012).

Exasperated at the airline's behavior, Carroll wrote a song titled "United Breaks Guitars." He filmed a music video for this song, which was uploaded to YouTube on July 6, 2009 (https://www.youtube.com/watch?v=5YGc4zOq ozo). This video "amassed 150,000 views within one day; it garnered over half a million hits by July 9, 5 million by mid-August 2009, 10 million by February 2011, and 14 million by February 2015" ("United Breaks Guitars," 2015). Carroll estimated that by 2012 his video had reached 150 million people. His story "was featured on BBC, CNN, and all major U.S. broadcast networks." He appeared on ABC's *The View* and Oprah Radio, and in *The New York Times*, *Rolling Stone*, and even *Reader's Digest* (Carroll, 2012). Another indication of the potential influence of this music video is the fact that in September of 2009 (shortly after its July release), a Google search for "United Breaks Guitars" found over 20 million hits. The fallout from this incident had significant negative effects on the company: "The BBC reported that United's stock price dropped by 10% within three to four weeks of the release of the video – a decrease in valuation of $180 million" (Sentium Strategic Communication, 2021). Clearly, this YouTube music video merits scholarly attention. Delbert and Benoit (2014) reviewed research on music as rhetoric and investigated two instances of persuasive attack in music. This section will critically analyze this music video as an instance of persuasive attack.

In the video, Carroll played his "United Breaks Guitars" with other footage edited into the video. His band members were dressed as a mariachi band member complete with sombreros. The video showed people dressed as baggage handlers throwing a guitar case back and forth.Other clips portrayed various United employees who fielded (or ignored) his complaints. This music video leveled two basic criticisms of United Airlines. These two accusations are summarized in a repeated refrain in the song:

You broke it, you should fix it.
You're liable, just admit it.

The airline damaged his guitar (a Taylor guitar, an expensive instrument). However, United refused to accept responsibility for the damage caused by its employees and reimburse Carroll for that damage.

The first accusation is advanced in several ways. First, as just noted, the song explicitly declared – repeatedly – that United broke his guitar. The title of the song and video also made this claim. The lyrics also stated that his Taylor guitar had "been the victim of a vicious act of malice at O'Hare" Airport in Chicago (some viewers might have known the high cost of Taylor guitars, which would implement the strategy of extent of the harm). The video reinforced this attack in several ways. Carroll was shown several times holding a guitar with an obviously broken headstock. Several clips portrayed baggage handlers throwing around guitar cases. One clip depicted a baggage handler who was thrown a guitar case but who missed the catch; the throw was not even close and then the "pitcher" pointed to himself as if to say "My bad for missing it." Another clip showed a guitar lying on the tarmac, portrayed as a victim with a chalk outline of the broken instrument (a crime scene investigator makes a brief appearance here). Carroll was also shown on the tarmac "playing" a guitar with a broken headstock as handlers behind him threw guitars back and forth. In one scene, a baggage handler wound up before throwing the case, evoking the way an athlete throws a shot put. One video clip showed the band behind the guitar displayed in a case on a stand, evoking the idea of a body in a casket. The three band members took off their sombreros as people might remove their hats at a funeral.

The video also offers several points about the second accusation, United's stonewalling of Carroll, was characterized in the song as a persistent or repeated offense. The video portrayed women dressed as flight attendants ignoring Carroll's attempts to check on his guitar: They "showed complete indifference." One of these flight attendants put her hands over her ears to shut out his complaint. He also sang about "a year-long saga of 'Pass the buck,' 'Don't ask me,' and 'I'm sorry sir your claim can go nowhere.'" Similarly, the song alluded to "all the airline's people, from New York to New Delhi" who stonewalled Carroll. The lyrics called out "Ms. Irlweg," portrayed in the video as a woman wearing this name tag, "who says the final word from them is 'no.'" The refrain declared, ironically, "Some big help you are." Carroll laments that "I should have flown with someone else or gone by car," rather than fly United, because "United breaks guitars." So, both of these criticisms were supported by words and video in this YouTube clip.

Notably, the year before the guitar video (2008) appeared, United Airlines had the second largest number of complaints among U.S. airlines (Bowen, 2009). This abysmal record likely meant that complaints against United, such as this one, would probably sound plausible to many viewers. The criticisms were well-developed in both the lyrics and the video. This attack is not complicated or difficult to understand: "You broke it, you should fix it. You're liable, just admit it." These attacks were developed humorously. For example, the low-budget video showed a model airplane on a stick moving to illustrate the journey. The sombrero-wearing mariachis and the guitar-shaped chalk outline keep the video light. Carroll was obviously unhappy, but he appeared more sad than angry (his criticisms never appeared vicious), which might have enhanced his credibility and strengthened the attack. This is a clear example of an effective persuasive attack that went viral with disastrous consequences for a company, as noted above. This was not the last time United faced criticism for misbehavior: Video of a passenger dragged off a United Airlines flight on April 9, 2017, went viral (Benoit, 2018).

## Persuasive Attack in Poetry

Poetry is another form of discourse that includes persuasive attack: Poems can employ ridicule, satire, or attacks (e.g., Previte-Orton, 2019). Actor John Lithgow (e.g., "Third Rock from the Sun" TV series) has written three books of poetry, perhaps best classified as doggerel. In these poems, he criticized Donald Trump, his associates, other politicians, and other people (Lithgow, 2019, 2020, 2021). This section will illustrate how persuasive attack occurs in poetry.

Lithgow criticized Donald Trump's proposed wall on the Southern border of the United States:

> Trumpty Dumpty wanted a wall,
> To stir up a rabid political brawl...
>     Dumpty's wall made no earthly sense,
> A boondoggle built at enormous expense.
> But he promised, in speeches despotic and shrill,
> He'd make certain that Mexico footed the bill (2019, p. 11).

The verse focuses on the President's policies. It advances two criticisms of the target: that he wanted to build a wall and that he would make Mexico pay for it. It hints at extensiveness ("enormous expense"). It also touches lightly on character, suggesting that he possessed the characteristics of a despot.

Lithgow lambastes Trump's national security advisor (2016-2017), Michael Flynn. Alluding to the opera Pinafore (by Gilbert and Sullivan), he wrote that:

> In spite of all my service in Afghani-stan afore,
> No one has screwed the pooch as much as Michael Flynn-afore (2019, p. 17).

This attack exemplifies the strategy of extent ("no one has screwed the pooch as much)" and illustrates the strategy of guilt by association (Trump having chosen Flynn). Lithgow reaches a bit to create a rhyme ("Flynn-afore"). The President's wisdom in political appointments is also questioned in a poem about Supreme Court justice nominee Brett Kavanaugh:

> Of all the fine judges that POTUS [President of the US] could choose
> To sit in the company of Charles Evans Hughes
> And Warren and Brennan and Brandeis and Marshall,
> Magisterial jurists, wise and impartial,
>     Instead, Dumpty fingered this callow young cad,
> The feeblest justice we'll ever have had,
> Hardly the Solon our Founders foresaw,
> He's Brett Kavanaugh (2021, p. 56).

This criticism uses both guilt by contrast (listing other, better justices) and extent ("feeblest justice") as it ultimately indicts President Trump's judgment.

> The author of this verse also attacked one of the President's lawyers, Rudy Giuliani, declaring that
> What goes on with Rapid Rudy,
> Monster of ineptitudy? (Lithgow, 2020, p. 12).

This attack takes poetic license with the word "ineptitude" to create a rhyme. Lithgow quite straightforwardly indicts Giuliani's competence and, indirectly, President Trump's judgment for relying on Giuliani.

These attacks also illustrate the strategy that an offensive act was repeated to increase its offensiveness. In one poem, Lithgow explored the idea that the President sought a sobriquet (such as "Alexander the Great"). He then offered two possibilities:

A POTUS whose pants are routinely on fire
Could be Dumpty the Huckster or Dumpty the Liar (2020, p. 103).

This criticism suggests that the President lied repeatedly. In another verse, President Trump is attacked for having fired five federal government Inspectors General:

In sum, *five inspectors* were given the can,
As Dumpty pursued his nefarious plan.
In the midst of a violent viral eruption,
No one was left to inspect his corruption (2020, p. 83; emphasis original).

Lithgow italicizes "*five inspectors*" to make certain readers of his verse would see that the fact that the President committed this offense repeatedly. It also suggests that the target benefitted from these offensive acts (responsibility) because he is accused of committing these offenses in order to protect his corruption from exposure.

Limericks can also be used as a vehicle for persuasive attack. Senator Ted Cruz was the object of ridicule because, during a winter storm with a power outage in Texas, he took his family on a vacation to Cancun. When called on for deserting his constituents, he indicated that he took the trip for his daughters. In 2021, Cruz alluded to a limerick in a tweet about President Biden. Some decided to give him a taste of his own medicine.

There once was a small "man" named Ted.
Who in a crisis to Mexico fled.
He said with a smirk
Because he's a terrible jerk
"Don't blame me, blame my daughters instead."

This poem attacks the Senator on multiple grounds. It suggests that he was a small man, that he fled to Mexico during a crisis, that he was a jerk, and that he blamed his daughters for his Cancun trip (ElectoralVote.com, 2021).

These examples show how persuasive attack occurs in poetry. Poetic attacks can be directed at both policy and character. These examples illustrate several strategies: extent, repeated offenses, guilt by contrast, and the accused benefitted from the attack.

# Persuasive Attack on Late Night Television

Late-night television, such as "The Late Show with Stephen Colbert" or "Jimmy Kimmel Live!," is a source of entertainment for many people. "Using full-season Live+7 ratings from Nielsen, Colbert comfortably won the spot with a total average of 2.95 million viewers..., while "Jimmy Kimmel Live!" beat NBC's "The Tonight Show" in total viewers, with 1.75 million to 1.54 million (White, 2021).

Over six million people watched the top three late-night television shows. The humor featured in these shows is frequently delivered in the form of ridicule (constituting persuasive attack). The large size of late-night television audiences creates an opportunity for substantial persuasive effects from these messages. Furthermore, this genre of television has resulted in effects in the real world. Segal (2015) argued that "The Daily Show" has affected public policy, giving several examples of legislative influence, including 9/11 first responders and families, health care for veterans, and net neutrality. Others have concurred, explaining that "Oliver's comedic commentary has been credited with helping influence US legislation, regulations, court rulings, and other aspects of US culture; this influence has been dubbed 'The John Oliver effect'" ("John Oliver," see also Luckerson, 2015; Dekel, 2015). Late-night television is a form of message that merits our attention.

## John Oliver Attacks Tucker Carlson

John Oliver, host of "Last Week Tonight," attacked Tucker Carlson (2021) in one segment. For example, Oliver ridiculed Carlson for being "a man who spends 85% of his time making the befuddled face of a thirteenth-century farmer learning about bitcoin." Most of the episode concerned Carlson's alleged embrace of white supremacy. Video from Carlson complained that his show was not on the air for six months before there was an organized and highly aggressive campaign by prominent democrats to denounce them as white supremacists. The first time it happened, the people who work on this show, many of them kids, were shocked and horrified by that. White supremacists? What's worse than that? The phrase evokes images of burning crosses and lynchings. It's awful (all quotations in this section are taken from Oliver, 2021).

Oliver responds to Carlson's statement with ridicule: "I'm so sorry, Tucker. I didn't realize your show was staffed entirely by children [Oliver exaggerates here; Carlson said many, but not all of those who worked on his show, were kids]. I never intended for them to get caught up in this. So my sincere apologies, you tiny little rascals." Oliver also employed *reductio ad absurdum* to attack Carlson's statement:

> "I don't burn crosses or lynch people, so I can't be a white supremacist" is a pretty weak argument. It's like saying "I can't be an anti-Semite because I didn't do the holocaust...." here is more than one way to be a terrible person. And Tucker — conveniently for him — doesn't fit neatly into a lot of people's perception of "white supremacist." Especially if they share his definition, that it must require burning crosses, Klan hoods, and a name tag that says "hello, my name is a racist." You might even have friends who think, "Tucker can't be racist. I've never heard him say the "n-word," as if that is the f*cking bar. (2021)

Oliver also suggests that minorities suffer more than those who were denounced as White supremacists: "I'm pretty sure black people are less terrified of being 'belittled' than of being killed, jailed, economically exploited, or indeed, denied access to healthcare after their heads literally explode from hearing someone in a bow tie and plaid blazer suggest being called racist is as bad as actually experiencing racism" [Oliver alludes to Carlson's customary dress here]. These excerpts illustrate how John Oliver deployed persuasive attack on his television show.

## Stephen Colbert Attacks Equifax

Stephen Colbert hosts "The Late Show with Stephen Colbert" (renamed "A Late Show with Stephen Colbert" during the pandemic). In September 2017, Equifax revealed that it had been hacked. Equifax is one of the three national credit bureaus, along with TransUnion and Experian. O'Brien (2017) reported that this "data breach is one of the worst ever, by its reach and by the kind of information exposed to the public." Colbert attacked the company later that month, reporting that Equifax's poor security "exposed 143 million people to identity theft. That means half the U.S. population could have had their identity stolen" (all quotations from Colbert's attack are taken from Colbert, 2017). This attack exemplified the strategy of stressing the extent of the problem. Colbert also noted that the company's misdeed was repeated, increasing the target's responsibility: They never reported that "they suffered another hack five months earlier, which involved the same intruders." This kind of repeated behavior hardly gives confidence in this company.

He also impugned the character of the company's executives: "Three Equifax managers sold company stock before the cyber-attack was revealed." He ridiculed this with a comparison between Equifax executives and airline pilots: "Ladies and gentlemen, pay no attention to these mountains we're rapidly approaching. The co-pilot and I are going to keep everyone safe by stepping outside and making sure these parachutes still work." Equifax executives profited from their inadequate computer security, adding insult to injury.

Furthermore, Colbert criticized the company for yet another misdeed. Individuals who wanted to safeguard their credit rating could set up a credit freeze. However, people who tried to establish credit "freezes through Equifax discovered that they had to pay Equifax for the privilege of protecting themselves." He related this to protection rackets: "They made you pay them to protect you from them. That's not a credit rating agency; that's the Mafia." He continued this idea with a fake slogan: "Equifax: Nice credit rating you got here, be a real shame if something happened to it." The argument here is that Equifax profited from the breaches they allowed. So, Colbert mounted a strong persuasive attack on Equifax in this episode of *The Late Show with Stephen Colbert*.

## Persuasive Attack in Tabloid Newspapers

Tabloid journalism is "largely sensationalist journalism (usually dramatized and sometimes unverifiable or even blatantly false)" ("Tabloid Journalism," 2021). These publications are sometimes labeled "supermarket tabloids" because they are often sold at the checkout counter in grocery stores (in fact, this section of the chapter was inspired after seeing these papers while checking out a supermarket order). The *National Enquirer*, for example, reached over 250,000 people in 2018 (*National Enquirer*, 2021), indicating a large audience reach. This analysis looked for examples of persuasive attacks over a six-month period in two tabloids: *The Globe* (2021) and the *National Enquirer* (2021). The articles in these publications are relatively short, ranging from a paragraph to a few pages (usually published with multiple pictures). As just noted, accusations in tabloids can be "unverifiable or even blatantly false"; therefore, there is no reason to believe any of these attacks are true. However, they do illustrate how attacks are made in such publications.

## Extent of the Harm

Unsurprisingly, given that these attacks occurred in sensationalist tabloid stories, the strategy of extensiveness was widely used. For example, one article indicated that Bill and Hillary Clinton had committed many murders: "The body count of anyone brave enough to cross the Clinton corruption machine has climbed to a staggering 69" ("Clinton Death Count Climbs," 2016, p. 8). This attack emphasizes the extent of the harm. Queen Victoria was called "an insatiable sexpot" ("Queen Victoria," 2016, p. 9), suggesting extensive sexual escapades. The *National Enquirer* declared that Hillary Clinton "is a compulsive, pathological, serial liar. She's been embellishing for the last 40 years, covering up corruption, erasing unflattering incidents, and making up self-congratulatory fake stories about herself" ("10 Reasons," p. 34). The story indicated that the breadth of her misbehavior was breathtaking. These excerpts show how tabloid articles employ accusations of extent in attacks.

## Repeated Offenses

A related strategy is declaring that an offense occurred repeatedly (of course, an extremely harmful act need not be repeated to be offensive). Pink Floyd's keyboard player, Rick Wright, was accused of multiple offenses: "Skirt-chasing Pink Floyd keyboard whiz Rick White was a druggie who constantly cheated on his wife Franka, and, after knocking up a groupie, pleaded poverty at their divorce, leaving her broke" ("Pink Floyd," 2016, p. 42). This attack identified several offenses, one of which was committed repeatedly ("constantly cheated"). *The Globe* characterized Bill Clinton as a "serial cheater" ("Bill Stabs Hillary," 2017, p. 6). The attack indicated that Clinton cheated chronically. Another article reported that, according to Moira Smith, Clarence Thomas "groped her bottom – repeatedly" ("Creepy Clarence, 2016, p. 57). Groping another person is bad enough, but repeated groping is worse. Actor Corey Sligh was reported to be "a twisted monster who preyed on an 8-year-old girl relative" ("Soaper Slapped," 2016). As if this offense were not bad enough, the article alleged that he "assaulted the girl several times in Florida and Georgia from April 1 to September 24" (p. 20). Pop singer Michael Jackson was also subjected to criticism in a tabloid newspaper: The pop star was depicted as having paid off "at least 20 underage boys, who were victims of his sick sexual cravings" ("Molester Michael," 2016, p. 42). A single act can be wrong, but when it is repeated, the behavior is even more offensive.

## Point to a Particularly Heinous Act

Michael Jackson was also accused of committing an especially offensive act. This pop star was accused of "sexually attacking" a girl "when she was just 12 – and paying her $900,000 to keep quiet" ("Molester Michael," 2016, p. 42). If true, this behavior is horrible and the *Globe's* description of his actions (not quoted here) was graphic and offensive. Tabloid journalism, not surprisingly, uses persuasive attack in its sensationalistic stories.

# President Barack Obama's Speech Against President Donald Trump

Former presidents try to avoid criticizing the current president: Such statements are rare but not completely unheard of. Quigley explained that "Former presidents being critical of the president … is pretty unusual" (2017; quoting George Edwards). Similarly, Lajka reported that "Historically, recent presidents do not attack sitting presidents that often" (2020, based on Peter Loge). President Barack Obama refrained from criticizing President Donald Trump for most of the latter's term in office, but the Democrat gave a speech attacking Trump (and acclaiming candidate Biden) near the end of the 2020 presidential campaign (on October 20) in Pennsylvania. This speech illustrated several strategies of persuasive attack: Obama asserted that Trump "hasn't shown any interest in doing the work or helping anybody but himself and his friends or treating the presidency like a reality show that he can use to get attention. And by the way, even then his TV ratings are down" (all quotations from Obama, 2016). This statement made three criticisms: Trump was not interested in doing the work of being president, he sought to help himself and his friends, and, despite his desire to gain attention, his ratings have dropped. President Trump's lack of leadership on the pandemic resulted in "lives lost" and "an economy that doesn't work." Deaths and a faltering economy from an inadequate response to Covid-19 are very offensive. Obama's speech illustrates several strategies for intensifying his attack against Trump, including extent, effects on the audience, and repeated offenses.

## Extent of Damage

President Obama used the strategy of extent of damage in several of his attacks on President Trump. For example, he observed that "The rest of us have had to live with the consequences of him proving himself incapable of taking the job seriously. At least 220,000 Americans have died. More than 100,000 small businesses have closed. Millions of jobs are gone. Our proud reputation around the world is in tatters." Certainly, 220,000 deaths, 100,000 business closings, millions of jobs lost, and America's reputation "in tatters" are significant effects. Similarly, Biden argued that "Trump won't even extend relief to the millions of families who are having trouble paying the rent or putting food on the table because of this pandemic." Obviously, millions of families suffering is a huge problem. The speech declared that Trump was "the first president since Herbert Hoover to actually lose jobs." Hoover served as president from 1929-1933 during the "Great Depression." President Obama pointed out that Korea's "per capita death toll is just 1.3% of what ours is. In Canada, it's just 39% of what ours is. Other countries are still struggling with the pandemic, but they're not doing as bad as we are because they've got a government that's actually been paying attention." The pandemic was raging more in the U.S. than other countries because of President Trump's lack of leadership. An unusual variant of enhancing an accusation by stressing the extent of the offense occurs when Obama stated that "His first year in the White House he only paid $750 in federal income tax." The President paid an exceptionally small amount of taxes.

## Effects on the Audience

The former president also intensified his attack on Donald Trump by pointing out the effects on his audience. Trump paid $750 in taxes in his first year in office; they likely paid far more: "How many people here pay less than that? It's just possible now that if you are living high on the hog and you only pay $750 in taxes that maybe, just maybe he might not know what work-ing people are going through here in Pennsylvania." Obama also lamented current conditions for those who need help: "the waitress trying to raise her kid on her own, the student trying to figure out how to pay for next semes-ter's classes, the shift worker who's always on the edge of getting laid off, the cancer survivor who's worried about her preexisting conditions, protections being taken away." Obama also observed that the Republicans have "attacked the Affordable Care Act at every turn, driving up costs, driving up the unin-sured. Now, they're trying to dismantle your care in the Supreme court as we speak as quickly as they can in the middle of a pandemic with nothing but empty promises to take its place. It's shameful. The idea that you would take healthcare away from people at the very moment where people need it most, what is the logic of that?" He related these offensive acts to the audience saying, "they're trying to dismantle your care." This speech pointed out how problems hurt people in his audience.

President Obama also criticized President Trump's poor choices in his appointments to the Executive Branch:

> His appointees are doing [harm] all across the government, actions that affect your lives. The Environmental Protection Agency that's supposed to protect our air and our water is right now run by an energy lobbyist that gives polluters free reign to dump unlimited poison into our air and water. The Labor Department that's supposed to protect workers and their rights, right now it's run by a corporate lobbyist who's declared war on workers, guts protections to keep essential folks safe during a pandemic, makes it easier for big corporations to shortchange them on their wages. The Interior Department, that's supposed to protect our public lands and wild spaces, our wildlife and our wilderness. And right now that's run by an oil lobbyist who's determined to sell them to the highest bidder. You've got the Education Department that's supposed to give every kid a chance, and that's run by a billionaire who guts rules designed to protect students from getting ripped off by for profit colleges and stiffs arm students looking for loan relief in the middle of an economic collapse. I mean, the person who runs Medicaid right now is doing their best to kick people off of Medicaid instead of sign them up for Medicaid.

He begins this passage by pointing out that these agencies "affect your lives." When discussing the EPA (Environmental Protection Agency), he explained that this agency was intended to "protect our air and water." He also mentions "our public lands... our wildlife and our wilderness." He relates these outrages to his audience. Notice that Obama also uses extent in this quotation by referring to "unlimited poison" from pollution.

## Repeated

President Obama lamented the fact that politicians' lies occur over and over: "Our democracy is not going to work if the people who are supposed to be our leaders lie every day and just make things up. And we've just become numb to it. We've just become immune to it. Every single day, fact checkers can't keep up." The idea that "fact checkers can't keep up" with the lies highlights the idea that these offensive acts are repeated.

# Attacks in Comparative Advertising

Attacks can also be found in commercial advertising. Ads and commercials usually tout the benefits of the sponsored goods or services. However, some advertisements identify flaws in or drawbacks to competitors: These kinds of advertisements are known as comparative ads because they compare the two products or services (see, e.g., Beard, 2010, 2018). Beard (2013) found that "both implied and explicit comparative advertising played important roles in the history of advertising throughout the twentieth century" (p. 190). Comparative advertising in magazines existed at the turn of the century but was relatively rare: "magazine advertisers rarely mentioned a competitor by name, with only 2% and 1% of ads in the 1900s and 1910s, and none in the 1920s" (p. 122). Comparative advertising, with criticism of competitors, became more common in the last few decades. This section does not seek out a sample of persuasive attacks in comparative advertisements; rather, it supports the claims that criticism can be found in commercial advertising.

Benoit (1995) concerned defenses to attacks. However, the chapter on the "Cola Wars" identified criticisms in advertisements sponsored by Coca-Cola and Pepsi-Cola in *Nation's Restaurant News*, a trade publication that circulates to restaurants and fast-food outlets. Although investigating strategies for intensifying attacks was not the purpose of this chapter, nevertheless some of these ads discussed illustrate strategies for intensifying attacks. For example, ads from Coke used extensiveness to criticize Pepsi: Coke outsells Pepsi by almost two to one, Diet Coke outsells Diet Pepsi by two to one, and Sprite outsells Slice nine to one. Coke also argued that, unlike Coca-Cola, Pepsi owns restaurants (e.g., Taco Bell, Pizza Hut, Kentucky Fried Chicken). Pepsi had invested $800 million in its fast-food franchises, arguing that when a restaurant bought Pepsi products, the profits Pepsi made helped finance competitors. One ad from Coke accused Pepsi of "fishing in your pond," an example of emphasizing effects on the audience (e.g., the restaurant owners and operators who subscribed to this trade publication, particularly Kentucky Fried Chicken, Pizza Hut, and Taco Bell). These ads were found in print (in magazines).

Benoit and Delbert (2010) investigated advertisements from Mac (Apple) attacking PC. These criticisms embraced PC's abilities (corresponding roughly to actions) – more susceptible to viruses and spyware – and its character – arrogant, mean, stressing image over substance. The commercials used personification, employing John Hodgman as the embodiment of the uptight PC and Justin Long representing the cool Mac. These attacks were found in video commercials.

## Persuasive Attack in Seventeenth Century English Broadside Ballads

We have seen in this chapter that songs promulgated via the Internet, such as "United Breaks Guitars," can function as persuasive attacks. However, Williams (2015) noted that "Broadside ballads were a uniquely powerful social tool that could educate a wide range of social classes, not only on current events and titillating gossip but also... political satire through music and performance" (p. 1). These songs were an important medium in the seventeenth century for several reasons. First, many people could not read at that time. As measured merely by the ability to sign one's name, about 30% of the men in seventeenth-century England could read (Melton, 2001; women had even lower literacy rates), which seems shockingly low today. This greatly limited the potential audience for written texts. In contrast, nearly everyone could hear these songs (except, of course, for those who were hearing impaired). Skeaping (2005) explained that "Broadside ballads were the pop songs of their day. Churned out in their thousands by anonymous hacks... they were whistled and sung in all walks of life" (p. 6). Second, lyrics are easier to remember than, for example, newspaper texts; the meter and rhymes, as well as their subject matter, made these ballads memorable. Repetition worked to drive home the ideas in these ballads (Benoit & Benoit, 2008; Cacioppo & Petty, 1983); ideas were repeated in choruses, and some songs were heard repeatedly by audiences. These ballads served as an important form of entertainment at a time without the Internet, cable television, radio, movies, and CDs. Rollins (2020) reported that "Ballads were, in the main, the equivalent of modern newspapers and... they performed their function as credibly in verse as the average newspaper does in prose. Journalistic ballads outnumbered all other types" (p. xi). Furthermore, the fact that many of these ballads were printed on sheets of paper enabled many (literate) minstrels to sing them at or about the same time, extending their potential influence. In fact, broadside ballads "were one of the most common forms of printed material between the sixteenth and nineteenth centuries, particularly in Britain, Ireland, and North America;" millions were printed ("Broadside Ballad," 2021). These songs merit scholarly attention.

The subjects of these ballads varied widely. However, it is clear that several of these songs can reasonably be considered instances of persuasive attack. This section will provide several illustrative examples of such criticism in these messages. These attacks proved a bit of a challenge to decipher because they used traditional spelling, as the excerpts below illustrate, and, for example, the letter s resembling an f, and the interchangeability of the letters u and v. An example from Wikicommons is reproduced below to illustrate these songs as printed ("An eighteenth century broadside ballad," 2021). Some of the published broadsheets included a woodcut illustration of the song.

The song "A warning for wives" levels several serious accusations against women generally:

> The story I now recite,
> Expounds you meanings evill
> Those women that in blood delight,
> Are ruled by the Devill,
> Else how can th' wife her husband kill,
> Or th' Mother her owne childs blood spill (spelling and punctuation original; Williams, 2015, pp. 105-06).

The last line exemplifies the strategy of obligation to protect. It would be horrible enough to kill any child, but to kill one's own offspring is even worse. Similarly, people should not ordinarily be expected to murder their spouses. Another song ("Witchcraft discovered and punished") vilified three old women who "joyn'd with Satan":

> So these Malicious Women, at the last,
> Having done mischiefs, were by Justice cast:
> For it appear'd they Children had destroy'd,
> Lamed Cattl, and the Aged much annoy'd.
> Having Familiars always at they beck,
> Their wicked rage on Mortals for to wreck:
> It being prov'd they used wicked Charms
> To murther men, and bring about sad harms (spelling and punctuation original; Williams, pp. 103-04).

These three women were accused of multiple offenses, including destroying children, laming cattle, and murdering men. This song concerned a specific English witch trial, in which three women (Temperance Lloyd, Mary Trembles, and Susannah Edwards) were tried, and then hanged, at the Exeter Assizes ("Bideford Witch Trial," 2021).

Another song dealt with the English Gunpowder Plot of 1605, singling out Robert Catesby, an English Catholic, for scorn. Explosives had been secreted in the House of Lords by Guy Fawkes (the foiling of this plot is celebrated in England as Guy Fawkes Day), but this threat was discovered and thwarted. This scheme was characterized in the song as "bloody treason," intending "to blow up both the King and Parliament" ("Gunpowder Plot," 2019). The idea here was to forcibly replace the Protestant government with a Catholic one.

Some of these songs enacted bawdy character assassination. One such song lampooned the Presbyterian Rump (a separate political faction formed in 1648 by Thomas Pride), making use of the multiple meanings of the word "rump." One song made "attacks on the Rump [which] invoked crude comparisons to buttocks productive only of smelly farts and turds" ("The re-resurrection of the Rump: Or, rebellion and tyranny revived"; Fumerton, 2020, p. 232). This is a clear example of political satire. One song ("The cucking of a scold") derided a woman who would scold others incessantly. In response, 100 archers and 100 soldiers (and 50 parrots!) "cucked" her in public (Rollins, 2020, p. 72). She was also tied to a chair and dunked into water. This was a terrible fate even for such an obnoxious person.

Another song ("The true reporte of the forme and shape of a monstrous Childe borne at Much Horkefsleye, a village three myles from Colchester, in the Countye of Essex, the xxi daye of Apryll in this yeare 1562") told of a deformed child. This child was "in want of honesty and excesse of sinne." The ballad sang of his evil, saying the "monster... shewes the sea of sinne," using the strategy of extent without resorting to numbers (Anonymous, 2012, p. 27). This child was reviled for being dishonest and sinful.

"Murder upon murder" recounts the misdeeds of Canburry Bess (aka Elizabeth Evans) and Country Tom (aka Thomas Sherwood), who killed three men: George Holt, Thomas Claxton, and Michael Lowe (Rollins, 2020).

Within three quarters of a yeare,
these murders they haue done,
,And maim'd and spoiled many a one, by their confession:
Such deadly blowes he did giue,
Twas strange that after [their deeds] they should liue (spelling original; Rollins, 2020, p. 436).

These two people killed and maimed time after time. Both were hanged for their repeated offenses. "The cries of the dead" (Rollins, 2020, p. 222; misspellings original) tells the story of a weaver, Richard Price, who had apprentices that he abused. The ballad recounts that he "tormented to death a boy of thirteene years old, with two others before." Price was said to have scourged the boy "day by day." The song recounted the nature of some of these assaults: "Never went they without brused and broken eyes, head and face blacke and blew." One lad had "one of his eares strooke off, woefully rent and torne." The fate of another was to have:

> His braines ny broken forth,
> and his neck burst in twaine,
> On his Limbs ouer all,
>     spotts of blood did remaine (spelling original, Rollins, 2020, p. 227).

The ballad not only indicated that the weaver's physical abuses were repeated, they were particularly heinous in nature, and the song suggests the victims were vulnerable (not only as 13-year-olds, but as apprentices under the control of their masters).

Some of these ballads contained political character assassination. They characterized people (non-politicians) uncharitably. Other ballads worked to expose wrongdoing, including a plot to blow up the government, a weaver's abuse of apprentices, wicked women who killed men and children, and serial killers. These ballads resemble the articles in tabloid newspapers discussed earlier, as they were often sensational and accompanied with photographs/illustrations (see also "Library of Congress," 2021).

## Attacks by the American Continental Congress on the British Parliament

The Declaration of Independence was proclaimed on July 4, 1776 (National Archives, 2021). One of the actions that provoked the American Revolution was the Tea Act, passed by the British Parliament in May of 1773. Three ships carrying tea, operated by the British East India Company, docked in Boston Harbor several months later: the *Dartmouth*, the *Beaver*, and the *Eleanor* (Boston Tea Party, 2009). On December 16, 1773, American colonists dressed as Native American Indians protested this tax by throwing 342 chests filled with tea from these vessels into the Boston Harbor. Subsequently, the Continental Congress held meetings in September 1774 in which they attacked the British Parliament in several documents (Continental Congress,

2018). This section recounts some of the criticisms leveled by the American colonists.

Most people have heard the cry of "No taxation without representation" raised by American colonists. However, their complaints went beyond this particular accusation. The Continental Congress lamented the fact that "Acts of Parliament have been passed... depriving the American subjects, in many instances, of the constitutional trial by jury" (p. 15). The Continental Congress also decried "attempts to take our property from us; to deprive us of that valuable right of trial by jury; to seize our persons, and carry us for trial to Great Britain; to blockade our ports; to destroy our Charters, and change our forms of government" (p. 37). This document argued that these actions were particularly offensive: "To enforce this unconstitutional and unjust scheme of taxation, every sense that the wisdom of our British ancestors had carefully erected against arbitrary power, has been violently thrown down in America, and the inestimable right of trial by jury taken away in cases that touch both life and property" (p. 32). So, the American colonies strongly attacked the British Parliament before they declared their independence. Attacks can be, and have been, leveled by one government against another.

## Observations and Conclusions

This chapter expands the scope of this investigation into persuasive attack. It shows how persuasive attack occurs in many contexts, from music videos, poetry, late-night television, tabloid newspapers, an unusual stump speech from a former President, comparative advertising, seventeenth-century ballads to colonial proclamations against Parliament. These attacks surface throughout human endeavor in a variety of media. This chapter illustrates persuasive attack in a variety of contexts to enhance our understanding of this important activity. These messages of criticism employed a variety of strategies for enhancing persuasive attack: extent, repeated offenses, guilt by contrast, effects on the audience, accused benefitted from the act, obligation to protect, and identifying a particularly heinous act.

# References

Anonymous. (2012). *A collection of seventy-nine blackletter ballads and broadsides: Printed in the reign of Queen Elizabeth, between the years 1559 and 1597. Accompanied with an introduction and illustrative notes.* Ulan Press.

An eighteenth century broadside ballad. (2021). *Wikipedia.* Accessed 9/11/21; https://en.wikipe dia.org/wiki/Broadside_ballad#/media/File:Tragical_Ballad_18th_century.png

Beard, F. (2010). Comparative advertising wars: An historical analysis of their causes and con-sequences. *Journal of Macromarketing. 30,* 270–286.

Beard, F. K. (2013). A history of comparative advertising in the United States. *Journalism & Communication Monographs, 15,* 114–216.

Beard, F. (2018). *Comparative advertising: History, theory, and practice.* Lexington Books.

Benoit, W. L. (1995). *Accounts, excuses, apologies: A theory of image restoration strategies.* Albany: State University of New York Press.

Benoit, W. L. (2018). Crisis and image repair at United Airlines: Fly the unfriendly skies. *Journal of International Crisis and Risk Communication Research, 1,* 11–26.

Benoit, W. L., & Benoit, P. J. (2008). *Persuasive messages: Balancing influence in communication.* Blackwell.

Benoit, W. L., & Delbert, J. (2010). "Get a Mac: Mac vs. PC TV Spots. *Relevant Rhetoric, 1.* Accessed 4/14/12: http://relevantrhetoric.com/wp-content/uploads/Get-A-Mac1.pdf.

Bideford witch trial. (2021). *Wikipedia.* Accessed 0/11/21: https://en.wikipedia.org/wiki/Bidef ord_witch_trial

Bill stabs Hillary in the back – again! (2017, January 9). *Globe,* pp. 6–7.

Boston Tea Party. (2009, October 27). Boston Tea Party. History.com. Accessed 9/22/21: https:// www.history.com/topics/american-revolution/boston-tea-party

Bowen, B. D. (2009). Airline quality rating 2009. *Purdue University e-Pubs.* Accessed 6/28/ 21: https://docs.lib.purdue.edu/cgi/viewcontent.cgi?article=1019&context=aqrr.

Broadside ballad. (2021). *Wikipedia.* Accessed 9/11/21: https://en.wikipedia.org/wiki/Broadside _ballad.

Cacioppo, J. T., & Petty, R. E. (1985). Central and peripheral routes to persuasion: The role of message repetition. In L. F. Alwitt & A. A. Mitchell (Eds.) *Psychological processes and advertising effects: Theory, research, and application* (pp. 91–111). Lawrence Erlbaum.

Carroll, D. (2012). *United breaks guitars: The power of one voice in the age of social media.* Hay House.

Clinton death count climbs: Mysterious new cases believed to be linked to Bill and Hillary. (2016, August 29). *National Enquirer,* p. 8.

Colbert, S. (2017, September 22). Equifax just Equi-F'ed everyone. Accessed 6/29/21: https:// www.youtube.com/watch?v=LyIEd5QVkyc

Creepy Clarence groped my butt! (2016, November 14). *Globe,* p. 57.

Dekel, J. (2015, February 18). "The John Oliver effect: How the Daily Show alum became the most trusted man in America." *National Post.* ISSN 1486-8008. Archived from the origi-nal on 27 July 2018. Retrieved 27 August 2015.

Delbert, J., & Benoit, W. L. (2014). Persuasive attack in music: A rhetorical analysis of "Fighting Trousers" and "The Very Model of a Mad Attorney General." *Relevant Rhetoric.* Accessed 6/27/21: http://relevantrhetoric.com/PersuasiveAttackinMusic.pdf.

Electoral-vote.com. (2021, November 19). This week in Schadenfreude. Accessed 11/19/ 21: https://www.electoral-vote.com/evp2021/Senate/Maps/Nov19.html#item-6

Fishbein, M., and Ajzen, I. (2010). *Predicting and changing behavior: The reasoned action approach.* Psychology Press.

Fumerton, P. (2020). *The broadside ballad in early modern England.* University of Pennsylvania Press.

Globe (tabloid). (2021). *Wikipedia.* Accessed 6/30/21: https://en.wikipedia.org/wiki/Globe_ (tabloid).

Gunpower plot. (2019, June 7). *History.com.* Accessed 9/11/21: https://www.history.com/topics/british-history/gunpowder-plot

John Oliver. (2021). Wikipedia. Accessed 6/26/21: https://en.wikipedia.org/wiki/John_Oliver.

Lajka, A. (2020, May 11). Obama is not the only president to criticize his successor. *AP.* Accessed 8/12/21: https://apnews.com/article/archive-fact-checking-8879101524

Lithgow, J. (2019). *Dumpty: The age of Trump in verse.* San Francisco, CA: Chronicle Prism.

Lithgow, J. (2020). *Trumpty Dumpty wanted a crown: Verses for a despotic age.* Chronicle Prism.

Lithgow, J. (2021). *A confederacy of Dumptys: Portraits of American scoundrels in verse.* Chronicle Prism.

Luckerson, V. (2015, January 20). "How the 'John Oliver Effect' Is Having a Real-Life Impact." *Time.* ISSN 0040-781X. OCLC 1311479. Archived from the original on 10 August 2015. Retrieved 28 August 2015.

Melton, J. V. H. (2001). *The rise of public enlightenment Europe.* Cambridge University Press.

Molester Michael paid me $900G in hush money! (2016, November 14). *Globe*, p. 42.

National Archives. (2021). Declaration of Independence. Accessed 9/22/21: https://www.archives.gov/founding-docs/declaration-transcript

National Enquirer. (2021). *Wikipedia.* Accessed 6/30/21: https://en.wikipedia.org/wiki/National_Enquirer

Obama. B. (2016, October 22). Barack Obama's scathing campaign speech. *CNN.* Accessed 10/22/20: https://www.cnn.com/2020/10/22/politics/obama-speech-transcript/index.html

O'Brien, S. A. (2017, September 8). Giant Equifax data breach: 143 million people could be affected. *CNN Business.* Accessed 6/29/21: https://money.cnn.com/2017/09/07/technology/business/equifax-data-breach/index.html

Oliver, J. (2021, March 14). Tucker Carlson: Last week tonight with John Oliver – transcript. *Scrapsfromtheloft.com.* Accessed 3/15/21: https://scrapsfromtheloft.com/2021/03/15/tucker-carlson-last-week-tonight-with-john-oliver-transcript/

Pink Floyd Rocker's dark side exposed! (2016, July 25). *Globe*, p. 42.

Previte-Orton, C. (2019). *Political satire in English poetry.* Wentworth Press.

Queen Victoria was secret sex machine. (2016, September 12). *Globe*, p. 9.

Quigley, A. (2017, May 9). Former presidents walk fine line in Trump's America: Trump's predecessors are trying to both defend their legacies and respect the unwritten rule of not undermining the current commander in chief. *Politico.* Accessed 8/12/21: https://www.politico.eu/article/former-presidents-walk-fine-line-in-trumps-america/

Rollins, H. E. (2020). *A Pepysian garland: Black-letter broadside ballads of thee years 1595–1639, chiefly from the collection of Samuel Pepys.* Alpha Editions.

Segal, C. (2015, August 6). 5 times "The Daily Show" actually in. fluenced policy. *PBS Newshour.* Accessed 6/26/21: https://www.pbs.org/newshour/arts/5-times-the-daily-show-influenced-policy

Sentium Strategic Communication. (2021). How saving $1,200 cost United Airlines 10,772,839 negative views on YouTube. *Marketing Rocket Fuel*. Accessed 6/27/21: https:// sentium.com/a-public-relations-disaster-how-saving-1200-cost-united-airlines-10772839-negative-views-on-youtube/

Skeaping, L. (2005). *Broadside ballads: Songs from the streets, taverns, theatres, and countryside of 17ᵗʰ century England*. Faber Music.

Soaper slapped with chilling kid molest [capitalized in red print] rap! (2016, December 26). *Globe*, p. 20.

Sons of Maxwell. (2009). United breaks guitars. Accessed 6/12/15: http://www.lyricsmode.com/ lyrics/s/sons_of_maxwell/united_breaks_guitars.html

Tabloid newspapers. (2021). *Wikipedia*. Accessed 6/30/21: https://en.wikipedia.org/wiki/Tabloid _journalism

Ten reasons Clinton should never be president. (2016, August 8). *National Enquirer*, pp. 34–35.

The Library of Congress Celebrates the Songs of America. (2021). *Library of Congress*. Accessed 9/16/21: https://www.loc.gov/collections/songs-of-america/articles-and-essays/musical-sty les/traditional-and-ethnic/traditional-ballads/

United Airlines statistics, passenger count, revenue totals and facts (2021). *DMR Business Statistics*. Accessed 6/27/21: https://expandedramblings.com/index.php/united-airlines-sta tistics-facts/

United Breaks Guitar. (2015). *Wikipedia*. Accessed 6/12/15: https://en.wikipedia.org/wiki/ United_Breaks_Guitars.

United States Continental Congress. (2018). *Extracts from the votes and proceedings of the American Continental Congress, held at Philadelphia, on the fifth of September, 1774*. Forgotten Books.

White, P. (2021, June 9). Late-night ratings: "The Late Show" wins season for fifth consecutive year as battle between Seth Meyers & James Corden heats up. *Deadline*. Accessed 6/27/ 21: https://deadline.com/2021/06/late-night-ratings-late-show-wins-season-fifth-consecut ive-year-1234772290/

Williams, S. F. (2015). *Damnable practices: Witches, dangerous women, and music in seventeenth-century English broadside ballads*. Routledge.

# Part VI
## TEACHING AND SCHOLARLY APPLICATIONS

The theory of persuasive attack is particularly relevant to students pursuing career options in public relations, politics, journalism, and a variety of other fields. Some students and scholars may view attack discourse with a certain level of disdain, and, at times, it can be an unnecessary, ill-timed, and completely unfair practice. However, persuasive attacks are also critical in the public sphere for drawing attention to harmful behaviors that warrant public scrutiny. Professional work in this area can position people on the side of crafting attack messages (e.g., political advertisers), whereas others (e.g., public relations managers) work to fend off attacks. This chapter is designed to help students on both sides know what key elements to look for when designing or evaluating an attack. These elements include: (1) classifying key strategies and understanding how they work together; (2) examining the timing of the attack and what role it plays in its effectiveness; (3) understanding who is the target of the attack and the relevant audiences for the messages; (4) determining the appropriate strength of language; and (5) looking at external evidence to gauge the effectiveness of the attack. Teachers may use this structure as a genesis point for developing resources to help students more fully understand these principles and better prepare them for professional environments.

# Classify Key Strategies and Understand How They Work Together

In creating an attack or evaluating one, a key component of the process is to determine what strategies are being used or should be used. In this book, several cases were explored to determine what strategies were present. For example, in the case of Adam LaRoche, the attacks increased negative perceptions of his actions by suggesting LaRoche was harming his son through his behavior and failing in his parental role. In this way, it functioned to simultaneously increase his responsibility for his behavior but also to emphasize the harm he was causing to his son's emotional development. Another example is William Thomas Steed's *Maiden Tribute of Babylon* newspaper series, which detailed the sex trafficking of children. His attacks also extensively used the strategy of increasing negative perceptions of the act by focusing on the specific harm done to these children. An important step in examining any case is to determine which strategies are at play.

It is also essential to determine how well the different strategies work together. For example, an attack is ineffective if it establishes responsibility for an act but not the offensiveness of it. Conversely, an attack will also fail if the offensiveness of the act is established, but not responsibility. With the Scot Peterson case, wherein he hid behind a building during the key moments of a tragic school shooting, the strategies fit together really well. He was derelict in his duty (despite being a trained resource officer); he was a coward at heart, which led to his inaction; the behavior itself was inherently harmful because it led to innocent victims being killed; and he made it worse by trying to portray himself as a victim. These strategies not only established responsibility and offensiveness but also demonstrated a flawed character, resulting in the ultimate damage to his image. In this case, strategies related to the act itself and the character of the accused were all present. However, in some cases, attacks only address one or the other—act or character. Benoit (2017) offers an important reminder from Aristotle that rhetoric is "enthymematic," meaning that not every component of an argument is overtly stated (p.13). Most of the time, the audience will participate in drawing a conclusion because one is not explicitly supplied by the researcher. Benoit (2017) elaborates on the connection between an enthymeme and the rhetoric of attack this way:

> The target audience may already accept some ideas (I would characterize them as beliefs or values) which are relevant to the rhetor's purpose. In this context, members

of the intended audience may already believe that a person (or group, or organization) possesses a trait – or may already accept the idea that a specific character trait is offensive. This means it is not always necessary to discuss both elements of a persuasive attack on character in a message: It may be enough to argue just that the target possesses an offensive character trait, or argue only that a particular character trait is offensive. Although both elements of persuasive attacks need not be present in a message, it is possible that the rhetor will discuss an idea already accepted by the audience in order to strengthen that idea. Nor is it necessary to use all four of the strategies for enhancing perceptions that a target possesses a trait, or necessary to use both strategies for increasing the perceived effectiveness of a character trait (p.13).

# Examine the Timing of the Attack and What Role it Plays in its Effectiveness

Another key element in understanding attacks is determining when the most appropriate time is to launch an attack. In the case of Soviet leader Nikita Khrushchev attacking the US government for its intrusive violation of sovereign Soviet territory, he levied his attack before most of the details of the U-2 crash were publicly revealed. At this point, US leaders had assumed that the pilot, Francis Gary Powers, had followed his instructions to destroy the surveillance devices on board the plane and to commit suicide, preventing information from leaking during any interrogations. However, what the United States did not know at the time was that the Soviets had captured Powers; he failed to destroy the equipment that had survived the crash and told his captors a number of details about the US surveillance mission. Unaware of these disclosures from Powers, the United States concocted a story about a National Aeronautics Space Administration (NASA) weather plane that had accidentally veered thousands of miles into Soviet airspace. The Soviets' strategy of attacking early while simultaneously omitting important details of the crash trapped the United States into an embarrassing fabrication. Here, the timing of the attack set up constraints on the United States that would likely alter any future strategies they would use to defend against the attack.

Often, attacks will come close to the time of the offense. Attackers usually waste little time when a situation arises that justifies an attack. The reason for this is that people are inherently very emotional, particularly when they feel personally offended by someone else's behavior. Charlie Sheen was obviously incensed after being fired from *Two and a Half Men* and was not likely going to wait long before going after producer Chuck Lorre and CBS executives. His purpose in offering the attack was to garner sympathy for himself and to turn the tide of public hostility against his bosses. The attack would have had less impact if he had waited until people had forgotten about the controversy and had moved on.

## Understand Who is the Target of the Attack and the Relevant Audiences

In many cases, there are different targets for an attack and different audiences who will listen to and respond to the attack. We cannot always classify an attack as effective or ineffective in general terms, but it is only effective for certain audiences. Additionally, some attacks stick better to one target than another. In the *Maiden Tribute of Modern Babylon* discourse, there were multiple targets of the attack, including parents who sold the victims, brothel-keepers who bought the victims, and a third group of villains who violated the victims. In the case of Scot "the coward from Broward" Peterson, the accusations naturally started with him due to his direct involvement in the event and then shifted to Sheriff Scott Israel, who merely supervised those who were tasked with responding.

The audience for an attack can also vary. One example is the *Blackfish* documentary, where the primary audience consisted of lay citizens who were unaware of the potential impact of the killer whale shows at SeaWorld. Stoking the fire of public rage was an effective tool for getting SeaWorld to stop the shows. Another example is Dave Carroll of the band Sons of Maxwell, who attacked United Airlines because the baggage crew broke his valuable guitars after throwing them around on the tarmac. After receiving the desired response from United itself, he knew he needed a larger audience and began sharing his story online through a song and music video written about the incident. His videos went viral and eventually did significant damage to the company's image (Andres, 2019; Finlay, 2023).

## Determine the Appropriate Strength of Language

Language choices also have to be carefully considered when offering or responding to an attack. In many ways, very strong and colorful language, especially words attacking a person's character, can really elevate the attack.

It can effectively demonize a person for misdeeds or maximize perceptions of the harm caused by that behavior. However, certain cases reveal that it can also be counterproductive if the attacker takes it too far. An example of this is Charlie Sheen's language choices, opting to call various individuals "maggots" and "aborted fetuses." This off-the-rails level of rhetoric stands in contrast to the case of Peterson's attackers, who called him a "coward," which seemed an appropriate descriptor at the time for most audiences following the news. Other appropriate language choices occurred during the *Blackfish* documentary, which used heightened language in the attack by suggesting the trainer was "scalped" and that killer whales would "rip you to shreds." These statements are no doubt colorful, but they do not seem to go beyond the normal bounds of attack under the circumstances because they are accurate descriptors.

## Look at External Evidence to Gauge the Effectiveness of the Attack

The last element for students and scholars to consider is the external evidence of the effectiveness or ineffectiveness of an attack. The previous elements discussed in this chapter require a keen examination of the strategies, timing, audience, and language, but often there are other forms of data that can be used to make judgments about attacks. Some of these include polling data, news commentary, and real-world negative harm to the perpetrator of an offense. For example, musician Dave Carroll's attacks on United Airlines led to a 10% decrease in its stock (a US$180 million loss). Although our chapter on late-night television hosts demonstrates an impact on public policy through their attacks, sometimes the attacks do not seem to create a long-term impact on the individuals being attacked. For example, John Oliver's attack on *Fox News* host Tucker Carlson, whom he accused of being a white supremacist, was fairly pointed at the time it was made, but it did not seem to have much impact on Carlson's ratings. This type of external evidence is sometimes helpful in gauging the effectiveness of an attack, but it should not be the only criterion for determining whether an attack is well-conceived and well-constructed.

The interplay between persuasive attack and defense is often dynamic. You might see an attack, then a defense, then more attacking based on the discourse of the initial defense. This makes it hard for people to examine cases in isolation because the attacks are often ongoing. Although the controversies surrounding accused sexual assaulters like Kevin Spacey, Harvey Weinstein, and Bill Cosby have died down in the press over the last few years, attacks against them will continue long into the future due to the heinous nature of the offense and the longevity of public memory in the digital world. Similar to the grotesque nature of the attacks surrounding child trafficking in London, these behaviors have resurfaced in the film *Sound of Freedom*. We are not suggesting these cases are not worthy of analysis the moment they happen, but we should keep in mind that our assessments of these contexts could change over time.

# References

Andres, T. (2019, July 5). A broken guitar, a YouTube video and a new era of customer service.

Benoit, W. L. (2017). Criticism of actions and character: Strategies for persuasive attack extended. *Relevant Rhetoric*, 8, 1–17.

Finlay, M. (2023, May 2). The story of Canadian musician Dave Carroll's anti-United Airlines protest songs. *Simple Flying*. https://simpleflying.com/dave-carroll-united-airlines-protest-songs/*Marketplace*. https://www.marketplace.org/2019/07/05/a-broken-guitar-a-youtube-video-and-a-new-era-of-customer-service/

# INDEX

www.ingramcontent.com/pod-product-compliance
Lightning Source LLC
Chambersburg PA
CBHW050649280326
41932CB00015B/2833